THE GAME OF GO

THE GAME OF

GO

THE NATIONAL GAME

OF JAPAN

BY ARTHUR SMITH

CHARLES E. TUTTLE COMPANY
RUTLAND, VERMONT & TOKYO, JAPAN

Published by the Charles E. Tuttle Company, Inc.
of Rutland, Vermont & Tokyo, Japan
with editorial offices at Suido 1-chome, 2-6, Bunkyo-ku, Tokyo, Japan

Copyright in Japan, 1956 by Charles E. Tuttle Co., Inc.

Library of Congress Catalog Card No. 56-12653
International Standard Book No. 0-8048-0202-5

Originally published, 1908
by Moffat, Yad & Company, New York

Tuttle edition
First printing, October, 1956
Thirty-eighth printing, 1994

PRINTED IN SINGAPORE

PUBLISHER'S NOTE

Arthur Smith, the author of the present volume, was one of the first Westerners ever to make a scientific study of Japan's ancient game of Go, and his classic work on the subject has never been surpassed for completeness, lucidity, and all-round excellence. First published in 1908, the book has been out of print these many years, while at the same time the growing interest in the game outside Japan has made it a rare and costly collector's item. We are pleased, then, to be able to make this excellent book once again available both for those who have already discovered the fascination of Go and for those who will find here their first introduction to the game that, in the opinion of many, ranks with chess as one of the world's best two-player games.

In order to preserve the full flavor of the original book, the present edition has been printed photographically from that of 1908, only the illustration facing page 22 having been replaced. Although a few of the author's topical remarks have become dated with the passing of years, the game itself has not changed and his explanations of its principles remain as uniquely excellent as on the day they were first written. For added convenience a glossary of Japanese terms has been inserted at the end of the volume.

Tokyo

PREFACE

This book is intended as a practical guide to the game of Go. It is especially designed to assist students of the game who have acquired a smattering of it in some way and who wish to investigate it further at their leisure.

As far as I know there is no work in the English language on the game of Go as played in Japan. There is an article on the Chinese game by Z. Volpicelli, in Vol. XXVI of the "Journal of the China Branch of the Royal Asiatic Society." This article I have not consulted. There is also a short description of the Japanese game in a work on "Korean Games with Notes on the Corresponding Games of China and Japan," by Stewart Culin, but this description would be of little practical use in learning to play the game.

There is, however, an exhaustive treatise on the game in German by O. Korschelt. This can be found in Parts 21–24 of the "Mittheilungen der deutschen Gesellschaft für Natur- und Völkerkunde Ostasiens." The student could readily learn the game from Herr Korschelt's article if it were available, but his work has not been translated, and it is obtainable only in a few libraries in this country. In the preparation of this book I have borrowed freely from Herr Korschelt's work, especially in the chapter devoted to the history of the game, and I have also adopted many of his illustrative games and problems.

Herr Korschelt was an excellent player, and acquired

his knowledge of the game from Murase Shuho, who was the best player in Japan at the time his article was written (about 1880).

My acquaintance with the game has been acquired from Mr. Mokichi Nakamura, a Japanese resident of this country, who is an excellent player, and whose enthusiasm for the game led me to attempt this book. Mr. Nakamura has also supplied much of the material which I have used in it. Toward the end I have had the expert assistance of Mr. Jihei Hashiguchi, with whom readers of the *New York Sun* are already acquainted.

Wherever possible I have given the Japanese words and phrases which are used in playing the game, and for those who are not familiar with the system of writing Japanese with Roman characters, I may say that the consonants have the sounds used in English, and the vowels the sounds that are used in Italian, all the final vowels being sounded. Thus, "dame" is pronounced as though spelled "dahmay."

NEW YORK, April, 1908.

INTRODUCTION

THE game of Go belongs to the class of games of which our Chess, though very dissimilar, is an example. It is played on a board, and is a game of pure skill, into which the element of chance does not enter; moreover, it is an exceedingly difficult game to learn, and no one can expect to acquire the most superficial knowledge of it without many hours of hard work. It is said in Japan that a player with ordinary aptitude for the game would have to play ten thousand games in order to attain professional rank of the lowest degree. When we think that it would take twenty-seven years to play ten thousand games at the rate of one game per day, we can get some idea of the Japanese estimate of its difficulty. The difficulty of the game and the remarkable amount of time and labor which it is necessary to expend in order to become even a moderately good player, are the reasons why Go has not spread to other countries since Japan has been opened to foreign intercourse. For the same reasons few foreigners who live there have become familiar with it.

On the other hand, its intense interest is attested by the following saying of the Japanese: "Go uchi wa oya no shini me ni mo awanu," which means that a man playing the game would not leave off even to be present at the death-bed of a parent. I have found that beginners in this country to whom I have shown the game always seem to find it interesting, although so far I have known no one who has progressed beyond the novice stage. The more it is played the more its beauties and opportunities for skill become apparent, and it may be unhesitatingly recommended to that part of the community, however small it may be, for whom games requiring skill and patience have an attraction.

It is natural to compare it with our Chess, and it may safely be said that Go has nothing to fear from the comparison. Indeed, it is not too much to say that it presents even greater opportunities for foresight and keen analysis.

The Japanese also play Chess, which they call "Shogi," but it is slightly different from our Chess, and their game has not been so well developed.

Go, on the other hand, has been zealously played and scientifically developed for centuries, and as will appear more at length in the chapter on the History of the Game, it has, during part of this time, been recognized and fostered by the government. Until recently a systematic treatment of the game, such as we are accustomed to in our books on Chess, has been lacking in Japan. A copious literature had been produced, but it consisted mostly of collections of illustrative and annotated games, and the Go masters seem to have had a desire to make their marginal annotations as brief as possible, in order to compel the beginner to go to the master for instruction and to learn the game only by hard practice.

Chess and Go are both in a sense military games, but the military tactics that are represented in Chess are of a past age, in which the king himself entered the conflict — his fall generally meaning the loss of the battle — and in which the victory or defeat was brought about by the courage of single noblemen rather than through the fighting of the common soldiers.

Go, on the other hand, is not merely a picture of a single battle like Chess, but of a whole campaign of a modern kind, in which the strategical movements of the masses in the end decide the victory. Battles occur in various parts of the board, and sometimes several are going on at the same time. Strong positions are besieged and captured, and whole armies are cut off from their line of communications and are taken prisoners unless they can fortify themselves in impregnable positions, and a far-reaching strategy alone assures the victory.

It is difficult to say which of the two games gives more pleasure. The combinations in Go suffer in comparison with those of Chess by reason of a certain monotony, because there are no pieces having different movements, and because the stones are not moved again after once being placed on the board. Also to a beginner the play, especially in the beginning of the game, seems vague; there are so many points on which the stones may be played, and the amount of territory obtainable by one move or the other seems hopelessly indefinite. This objection is more apparent than real, and as one's knowledge of the game grows, it becomes apparent that the first stones must be played with great care, and that there are certain definite, advantageous positions, which limit the player in his choice of moves, just as the recognized Chess openings guide our play in that game. Stones so played in the opening are called "Joseki" by the Japanese. Nevertheless, I think that in the early part of the game the play is somewhat indefinite for any player of ordinary skill. On the other hand, these considerations are balanced by the greater number of combinations and by the greater number of places on the board where conflicts take place. As a rule it may be said that two average players of about equal strength will find more pleasure in Go than in Chess, for in Chess it is almost certain that the first of two such players who loses a piece will lose the game, and further play is mostly an unsuccessful struggle against certain defeat. In Go, on the other hand, a severe loss does not by any means entail the loss of the game, for the player temporarily worsted can betake himself to another portion of the field where, for the most part unaffected by the reverse already suffered, he may gain a compensating advantage.

A peculiar charm of Go lies in the fact that through the so-called "Ko" an apparently severe loss may often be made a means of securing a decisive advantage in another portion of the board. A game is so much the more interesting the oftener the opportunities for victory or defeat change, and in Chess these chances do not change often, seldom more than twice. In Go, on the other hand, they change much more frequently, and sometimes just at the end of the game, perhaps in the last moments, an almost certain defeat may by some clever move be changed into a victory.

There is another respect in which Go is distinctly superior to Chess. That is in the system of handicapping. When handicaps are given in Chess, the whole opening is more or less spoiled, and the scale of handicaps, from the Bishop's Pawn to Queen's Rook, is not very accurate; and in one variation of the Muzio gambit, so far from being a handicap, it is really an advantage to the first player to give up the Queen's Knight. In Go, on the other hand, the handicaps are in a progressive scale of great accuracy, they have been given from the earliest times, and the openings with handicaps have been studied quite as much as those without handicaps.

In regard to the time required to play a game of Go, it may be said that ordinary players finish a game in an hour or two, but as in Chess, a championship game may be continued through several sittings, and may last eight or ten hours. There is on record, however, an authentic account of a game that was played for the championship at Yeddo during the Shogunate, which lasted continuously nine days and one night.

Before taking up a description of the board and stones and the rules of play, we will first outline a history of the game.

CONTENTS

I

HISTORY OF THE GAME

THE game of Go is probably the oldest of all known games. It was played by the Chinese from earliest antiquity, and has been played in its present form by the Japanese for over eleven centuries, but while the game originated in China, the Japanese have far surpassed the Chinese in skill at the game, and it has come to be regarded in Japan as their national game.

In the old Chinese works three persons are named as the originators of the game, but in Japan its invention is commonly attributed to only one of these. This man is the Chinese emperor Shun, who reigned from 2255 to 2206 B.C. It is said that this emperor invented the game in order to strengthen the weak mind of his son Shang Kiun. By others the invention of the game is attributed to the predecessor of Shun, the emperor Yao, who reigned from 2357 to 2256 B.C. If this theory is correct it would make the game about forty-two hundred years old. The third theory is that Wu, a vassal of the Chinese emperor Kieh Kwei (1818–1767 B.C.) invented the game of Go. To the same man is often attributed the invention of games of cards. It would seem that this last theory is the most credible, because it would make the invention more recent, and because the inventor is said to have been a vassal and not an emperor.

Whatever may be the truth in regard to the origin of the

game, it is perfectly certain that Go was already known in China in early antiquity. In old Chinese works, of which the oldest is dated about a thousand years before Christ, a game which can be easily recognized as Go is mentioned casually, so that at that time it must have been well known.

We are told also that in China somewhere about 200 B.C., poetry and Go went hand in hand, and were in high favor, and a poet, Bayu, who lived about the year 240 A.D., made himself famous through poems in which he sang the praises of the game.

It is remarkable that in the old books it is stated that in the year 300 A.D. a man by the name of Osan was so skilled in Go that he could take all the stones from the board after the game had been finished and then play it over from memory. This is of interest also as showing that in the course of time playing the game has had the effect of strengthening the memory of Go players, because there are now hundreds of players in Japan who can replace a game move for move after it has been disarranged. It is in fact the customary thing for a teacher of the game to play the game over in that way in order to criticise the moves made by the student.

Anecdotes have come down to us from the old Chinese times in regard to the game, of which we will mention only one, which shows how highly it was esteemed.

Sha An, a man who lived in the time of the Tsin Dynasty (265–419 A.D.), carried on a war with his nephew Sha Gen. Growing tired of taking life, they left the victory to be decided by a game of Go, which they played against each other.

The esteem in which players were held in the old Chinese times is also shown by the titles with which they were honored; to wit, "Kisei" or "Ki Shing," from "Ki," meaning Go, and "Sei," a holy man, and "Shing," magician or sage.

In the time of the Tang Dynasty (618–906 A.D.), and again during the Sung Dynasty (960–1126 A.D.), the first books about Go were written. The game then flourished in China, and there were then many distinguished players in that country.

According to the Japanese reckoning of time, Go was introduced into Japan in the period Tem pyo, during the reign of the emperor Shomu, which according to the Chinese records was the thirteenth year of the period Tien Tao, and during the reign of the emperor Huan Tsung. According to our calendar this would be about the year 735 A.D.

A man otherwise well known in the history of Japan, Kibi Daijin, was sent as an envoy to China in that year, and it is said that he brought the game back with him to Japan.

Go may have been known in Japan before that date, but at any rate it must have been known about this time, for in the seventh month of the tenth year of the period Tem pyo (A.D. 738), we are told that a Japanese nobleman named Kumoshi was playing Go with another nobleman named Adzumabito, and that in a quarrel resulting from the game Kumoshi killed Adzumabito with his sword.

On its introduction into Japan a new era opened in the development of the game, but at first it spread very slowly, and it is mentioned a hundred years later that the number of Go players among the nobility (and to them the knowledge of the game was entirely confined) was very small indeed.

In the period called Kasho (848–851 A.D.), and in Nin Ju (851–854 A.D.), a Japanese prince dwelt in China, and was there taught the game by the best player in China. The following anecdote is told in regard to this prince: that in order to do him honor the Chinese allowed him to meet the best players, and in order to cope with them he hit upon the idea of placing his stones exactly in the same way as those of his opponent; that is to say, when his opponent placed a stone at any point, he would place his stone on a point symmetrically opposite, and in that way he is said to have won. In regard to this anecdote it may be said that the Chinese must have been very weak players, or they would speedily have found means of overcoming this method of defense.

We next hear that in the year 850 a Japanese named Wakino became famous as a great devotee of the game. He played continuously day and night, and became so engrossed in the game that he forgot everything else absolutely.

In the next two centuries the knowledge of the game did not extend beyond the court at Kioto. Indeed, it appears that it was forbidden to play Go anywhere else than at court. At all events we are told that in the period called Otoku (1084–1087 A.D.) the Prince of Dewa, whose name was Kiowara no Mahira, secretly introduced the game into the province of Oshu, and played there with his vassals. From that time not only the number of the nobility who played the game increased rapidly, but the common people as well began to take it up.

There is also a story which comes down from the Kamakura period in regard to Hojo Yoshitoki. He is said to have been playing Go with a guest at the moment that news arrived of the uprising of Wada Yoshimori. Yoshitoki is said to have first finished the game in perfect calmness before he thought of his measures for subduing the revolution. This was in the first year of Kempo, or 1213 A.D.

In the beginning of the thirteenth century we find that Go was widely known in the samurai class, and was played with zeal. At that time everybody who went to war, from the most famous general down to the meanest soldier, played the game. The board and stones were carried with them to the field of battle, and as soon as the battle was over, they were brought out, and the friendly strife began. Many of the monks and poets of that period also had a taste for Go, and several of them are mentioned as celebrated Go players.

All three of the great Japanese generals, Nobunaga, Hideyoshi, and Iyeyasu, were devotees of the game. It is related that Nobunaga came to Kioto in the tenth year of Ten Sho, 1582 A.D., and lived in the Honnoji Temple. One night the celebrated Go player, Sansha, of whom more hereafter, came and played with him until midnight. Sansha had scarcely taken his departure when the uprising of Akechi Mitsuhide broke out.

In the periods Genki (1570–1572), Ten Sho (1573–1591) until Keicho (1596–1614), and Gen Wa (1615–1623), there were many celebrated players among the monks, poets, farmers and tradespeople. They were called to the courts of the daimios and to the halls of the nobles, either in order that the nobility might play with them, or more frequently merely to exhibit their skill at the game. This custom existed up to the time of the fall of the Shogunate.

That the Japanese could find pleasure in merely watching a game that is so abstract in its nature and so difficult to understand is evidence of the fact that they were then a highly cultivated people intellectually. We find nothing like it in this country except in the narrowest Chess circles.

In the beginning of the seventeenth century Go attained such a high development that there appeared a series of expert players who far surpassed anything known before. Of these the most famous were Honinbo Sansha Hoin, Nakamura Doseki, Hayashi Rigen, Inouye Inseki, and Yasui Santetsu.

Sansha was the son of a merchant of Kioto. When he was nine years old he shaved his head, named himself Nikkai, and became a Buddhist monk in the Temple of Shokokuji, which was one of the principal temples of the Nichi Ren sect in Kioto. From his early life Sansha was very skilful at the game, and upon giving up his profession as a monk, he obtained permission to institute a school of Go players, and he then took the name of Honinbo Sansha. He was on terms of familiar intercourse with Nobunaga, Hideyoshi and Iyeyasu, often accompanied them on their travels and campaigns, and was present at many of the battles of that troublous epoch.

The school of Go which Honinbo opened, however, was merely a private undertaking. The first State institution in which Go was taught was founded by Hideyoshi in the period Ten Sho (1573–1591), but it seems to have had a short existence, and the permanent institution which lasted until the fall of the Shogunate was founded by the

successor of Hideyoshi, Iyeyasu. Iyeyasu became Shogun
in the year 1603, and the foundation of the Go Academy
or "Go In," as the Japanese call it, must have occurred
soon after he ascended the throne. Honinbo Sansha, who
was still the best Go player in Japan, was named as
the head of the institution. The other most skilful masters
were installed as professors with good salaries. To Honinbo
Sansha, the director, was given 350 tsubo of land (a tsubo
is as big as two Japanese mats or tatami, and is therefore
six feet square), and an annual revenue of 200 koku of rice
(a koku is a little more than five bushels). Men of the best
intelligence could now dedicate themselves to the education
of students and the further development of the game, freed
from the cares of earning a livelihood. In both respects
the institute was eminently successful. Its graduates were
much more skilful than the previous generation of Go
players living in the land. They devoted themselves entirely to the game, and either found positions as players at
the court of a daimio, or traveled through the country
(like the poets and swordsmen of that period), playing the
game and giving instruction in its mysteries as they found
opportunity. If they came to a place which pleased them,
they often let their years of wandering come to an end and
remained there, making their living as teachers of the game.

At the time of the founding of the Academy, besides
Honinbo, the previously mentioned masters, Hayashi,
Inouye, and Yasui, were installed as professors. For some
reason, Nakamura, who is mentioned above as one of the
contemporaries of Honinbo, did not appear at the Academy.
Each of the four masters above named founded his school
or method of play independently of the others, and the cus-

tom existed that each teacher adopted his best pupil as a son, and thus had a successor at his death; so the teachers in the Academy were always named Honinbo, Inouye, Hayashi, and Yasui. (Lovers of Japanese prints are already familiar with this continued similarity of names.)

The best players of the Academy had to appear every year before the Shogun and play for his amusement. This ceremony was called "Go zen Go," which means "playing the game in the august presence," or "O shiro Go," "Shiro" meaning "the honorable palace," and the masters of the game entered these contests with the same determination that was displayed by the samurai on the field of battle.

An anecdote has come down to us from the reign of the third Shogun, Tokugawa Iyemitsu, showing how highly the Go masters regarded their art. At that time Yasui Sanchi was "Meijin," which, as we shall see in a moment, meant the highest rank in the Go world, while Honinbo Sanyetsu held the rank of "Jo zu," which was almost as high, but which, according to the rules, would entitle him to a handicap of one stone from his expert adversary; and these two men, being the best players, were selected to play in the Shogun's presence. Honinbo, feeling conscious of his skill, disdained to accept the handicap, and met his adversary on even terms. The game was proceeding in the presence of the court nobles before the Shogun had appeared, and among the spectators was Matsudaira Higo no Kami, one of the most powerful noblemen of that epoch. Yasui Sanchi was a favorite of Matsudaira and as he watched the play he remarked audibly that Honinbo would surely be defeated. Honinbo Sanyetsu heard the remark, and pausing in his play, he allowed the stone which he was about to place on the board to fall back into the "Go tsubo" or wooden jar that holds the Go stones, gently covered the "Go tsubo," and drawing himself up with great dignity, said: "I am serving the Shogun with the art of Go, and when we Go masters enter a contest, it is in the same spirit as warriors go upon the field of battle, staking our life, if necessary, to decide the contest. While we are doing this we do not allow interference or comments from any one, no matter how high may be his rank. Although I am not the greatest master of the game, I hold the degree of 'Jo zu,' and, therefore, there are few players in Japan who are able to appreciate my plans, tactics, or strategy. Nevertheless, the Prince of Higo has unwarrantedly prophesied my defeat. I do not understand why he has done this, but if such a comment were allowed to become a precedent, and onlookers were permitted to make whatever comments on the game they saw fit, it would be better that the custom of the 'O shiro Go' should cease." Having said this, he raised himself from his seat. At this moment the court officers announced the coming of the Shogun, and the noblemen who had assembled to see the contest, surprised and confused by the turn affairs had taken, earnestly persuaded Honinbo to reseat himself and continue the game. This he obstinately refused to do, and endeavored to leave the imperial chamber. Prince Matsudaira, taken aback, scarcely knew what to do. However, he kotowed to Honinbo and, profusely apologizing, besought the offended master to finish the contest. Honinbo Sanyetsu was appeased, and resumed his seat at the board, and both players, aroused by the incident, exerted every effort to achieve victory. Honinbo Sanyetsu won, whereupon the Prince of Higo was

greatly humiliated. Since then the name of Sanyetsu has
always been revered as one of the greatest of the Honinbo
family.

In the degenerate days toward the end of the Tokugawa
Dynasty the "Go zen Go" became a mere farce, and the
games were all played through and studied out beforehand,
in order that the ceremony in court might not last too long.
The custom was, however, maintained until the fall of the
Shogunate in 1868.

Honinbo Sansha established at the time of the foundation of the Academy a method of classifying the players
by giving them degrees, which still exists, although no
longer under the authority of the State. When a man
attained to a certain measure of skill in the game he received
the title "Shodan," or, of the first degree.   The still stronger
players were arranged as "Nidan," "Sandan," "Yodan,"
etc., or of the second, third, and fourth degrees.   The highest degree in the series was "Kudan," or the ninth degree.
In order to attain the first degree, or "Shodan," the candi-
date must be an excellent player, so good in fact that he
could follow the game as a profession. In other games
such a graduated system of classifying players would be
scarcely possible, but among good Go players it is
feasible, because the better player almost invariably wins,
even if he be but slightly superior. If the difference in
skill could not be equalized in some way the game would
become tiresome, as the weaker player would almost always
be able to foresee his defeat. The stronger player, therefore,
allows his adversary to place enough stones on the board
as a handicap to make the adversaries approximately equal.

According to the rules of the Academy, if the difference

between the skill of the players was only one degree, the weaker player would be allowed the first move. If the difference was two degrees, the weaker player would be allowed to place a stone on the board, and the stronger player would have the first move, and so on; in other words, the difference between each degree might be called half a stone. Thus, a player of the fourth degree would allow a player of the first degree to place two stones on the board as a handicap, but would have the first move. A player of the seventh degree would allow a player of the first degree three stones, and a player of the ninth degree would allow a player of the first degree four stones. Four was the highest handicap allowed among the players holding degrees, but, as we shall see later, among players of less skill greater handicaps are frequently given.

A player of the seventh degree also received the honorary title " Jo zu," or the higher hand. Those of the eighth rank were called "Kan shu," or the half-way step, and those of the ninth degree were called "Mei shu," the clear, bright hand, or "Mei jin," literally "celebrated man." It is related that this last appellation arose in the time of Nobunaga, who was a spectator of a game played by Honinbo Sansha with some contemporary, and who expressed his admiration of the skill of Honinbo by exclaiming "Mei jin!" which thus became the title applied to players of the highest skill.

Since the institution of this method of classifying Go players over three hundred years ago, there have been only nine players who have attained the ninth degree, and only fourteen players who have attained the eighth degree. On the other hand, there have been many more of the seventh, and many more still of each of the lower degrees. In 1880, at the time Korschelt wrote the article previously referred to, there was only one player in Japan holding the seventh degree, and that was the celebrated Murase Shuho. At present there is one player who holds the ninth degree. His name is Honinbo Shuyei, and he is the only player who has attained the ninth degree during the period called the "Meiji," or since the fall of the Shogunate forty years ago.

This arrangement of the players in degrees is unknown in China. and Korea. On the other hand, it is in use in the Ryukyu or Loochoo Islands.

The Japanese seem to have regarded the classification in degrees as an absolute standard of measurement. Nevertheless, it must necessarily have varied from time to time, and in the course of centuries the standard must gradually have risen.

Players of high rank who are challenged by the improving players of the lower grades will instinctively desire to make it more difficult for the new players to attain the higher degree, because their own fame, which is their highest possession, depends upon the result of the game; and assuming that all trial games could be conducted in an impartial and judicial spirit, nevertheless, all the players would become more expert from the hard practice, even if their skill in relation to each other remained the same.

Thus a seventh degree player of to-day would be better in a year although he still remained in the seventh degree, and this constant raising of the standard must lead us to suppose that a player of the seventh degree now is quite equal or perhaps superior to an eighth or ninth degree player of a hundred or two hundred years ago. As an illustration of this increase in skill, we only have to compare the standard set in the Ryukyu Islands. They also established the classification in degrees soon after the foundation of the Academy in Japan, and then the two institutions seem to have lost touch. Korschelt relates that for the first time about the year 1880 a Go player of the second degree from the Satsuma province visited those Islands and tried his skill with their best players, and found that he could easily defeat the players there classified as of the fifth degree.

The position as head of the Academy was much coveted by Go players, but it was generally held by the Honinbo family. One of the last incidents in relation to the Academy tells of an attempt on the part of Inouye Inseki, the eleventh of that line, to obtain the headship of the Academy when Honinbo Jowa, who was the twelfth Honinbo, retired. Inseki was afraid he could not obtain the coveted position by a contest, and therefore strove to obtain it by intrigue from the Shogun's officer intrusted with the business of the Academy. When Jowa retired he was not unaware of the desires of Inseki, but it did not trouble him much, as he felt confident that the fourteenth Honinbo, whose name was Shuwa, could successfully defend his title. However, at last matters came to such a point that Jowa ordered Shuwa to present a petition to the Shogun requesting that the title be settled by contest, but the Shogun's officer, who was in league with Inseki, returned the petition, whereupon all of the Honinbo house rose and insisted on their rights in accordance with custom and precedent, and at last their petition was granted. It was fixed that the title was to be decided by ten games, and the first

game began at the residence of the Shogun's officer, Inaba
Tango no Kami, on the 29th of November, in the eleventh
year of Tempo (about sixty-six years ago), and it ended
the same year on the 13th of December. There was an
adjournment of four days, and on one occasion the contest
lasted all night. Therefore in all it took nine days and one
night to finish the game.

It is unnecessary to say that both players put forth all
their efforts in this life and death struggle, and it is said
that Inseki's excitement was so intense as to cause blood
to gush from his mouth, but he finally lost by four stones,
and the other nine games were not played. Inseki, however, mortified by his defeat, again challenged Shuwa.
This game began on the 16th of May in the thirteenth year
of Tempo, and lasted two days. Inseki again lost by six
stones. On November 17th of the same year a third contest took place between Shuwa and Inseki in the presence
of the Shogun in his palace at Tokio. Inseki again lost by
four stones. In all these contests Inseki as the challenger
had the first move, and he finally became convinced of his
inability to win from the scion of the Honinbo family, and
abandoned his life-long desire, and it is related that thereupon the houses of Honinbo and Inouye became more
friendly than ever.

In the first half of the nineteenth century Go had a
period of great development. This occurred according to
the Japanese calendar in the periods called Bun Kwa (1804–
1818), Bun Sei (1818–1829), and Tempo (1830–1844).
The collection of specimen games of that time are to-day
regarded as models, and the methods of play and of opening
the game then in use are still studied, although they have

been somewhat superseded. The best games were played by the Honinbos Dosaku and Jowa and Yasui Sanchi.

On the fall of the Shogunate in the year 1868 the Go Academy came to an end, and with it the regulation of the game by the State. A few years later the daimios were dispossessed, and they did not feel an obligation as private individuals to retain the services of the Go players who had been in attendance at their courts. Thereupon ensued a sad time for the masters of the game, who had theretofore for the most part lived by the practice of their art, and to make things still worse, the Japanese people lost their interest in Go. Upon the opening of the country the people turned with enthusiasm to the foreigners. Foreign things were more prized than native things, and among the things of native origin the game of Go was neglected.

About the year 1880, however, a reaction set in; interest in the old national game was revived, and at the present day it is fostered with as much zeal as in the olden times.

Most of the higher officials of the government, and also the officers in the army and navy, are skilled players. The great daily newspapers of the capitals have a Go department, just as some of our periodicals have a department devoted to Chess, and the game is very much played at the hot springs and health resorts, and clubs, and teachers of the art are found in all of the larger cities. Go has always retained something of its early aristocratic character, and in fact, it is still regarded as necessary for a man of refinement to possess a certain skill at the game.

During the recent Russo-Japanese War the strategy employed by the Japanese commanders certainly suggested the methods of play used in the game of Go. Whether this was an accidental resemblance or not I cannot say. At Liao Yang it seemed as if Marshal Oyama had got three of the necessary stones advantageously placed, but the Russians escaped before the fourth could be moved into position. At the final battle of Mukden the enveloping strategy characteristic of the game was carried. out with still greater success.

At the present time the division into the four schools of Honinbo, Inouye, Hayashi, and Yasui, no longer exists, and Go players are divided into the schools of Honinbo and Hoyensha. This latter school was established about the year 1880 by Murase Shuho, to whom reference has already been made.

The Honinbo school is the successor of the old Academy, while the new school has made one or two innovations, one of the most fortunate being a rule that no game shall last longer than twenty-four hours without interruption. The Hoyensha school also recognized the degree "Inaka Shodan," which means the "first degree in the country," and is allowed to a class of players who are regarded as entitled to the first degree in their native town, but who are generally undeceived when they meet the recognized "Shodan" players of the metropolis.

While in Japan Go has attained such a high development, largely through the help of the government, as has been shown, it seems to be decadent in its motherland of China. The Japanese players assure us that there is no player in China equal to a Japanese player of the first degree. In Korea also the game is played, but the skill there attained is also immensely below the Japanese standard.

Having now given an idea of the importance of the game in the eyes of the Japanese, and the length of time it has been played, we will proceed to a description of the board and stones, and then take up the details of the play.

II

DESCRIPTION OF THE BOARD AND STONES

THE board, or "Go Ban" as it is called in Japanese, is a solid block of wood, about seventeen and a half inches long, sixteen inches broad, and generally about four or five inches thick. It has four detachable feet or legs so that as it stands on the floor it is about eight inches high. The board and feet are always stained yellow.

The best boards in Japan are made of a wood called "Kaya" (*Torreya Nucifera*) a species of yew. They are also made of a wood called "Icho" or Gingko (*Salisburia adiantifolia*) and of "Hinoki" (*Thuya Obtusa*) a kind of cedar. At all events they must be of hard wood, and yet not so hard as to be unpleasant to the touch when the stone is placed on the board, and the wood must further have the quality of resonance, because the Japanese enjoy hearing the sound made by the stone as it is played, and they always place it on the board with considerable force when space will permit. The Japanese expression for playing Go, to wit, "Go wo utsu," literally means to "strike" Go, referring to the impact of the stone. In Korea this feature is carried to such an extreme that wires are stretched beneath the board, so that as a stone is played a distinct musical sound is produced. The best boards should, of course, be free from knots, and the grain should run diagonally across them.

In the back of the board there is cut a square depression. The purpose of this is probably to make the block more resonant, although the old Japanese stories say that this depression was put there originally to receive the blood of the vanquished in case the excitement of the game led to a sanguinary conflict.

The legs of the board are said to be shaped to resemble the fruit of the plant called "Kuchinashi" or Cape Jessamine (*Gardenia floribunda*), the name of which plant by accident also means "without a mouth," and this is supposed to suggest to onlookers that they refrain from making comments on the game (a suggestion which all Chess players will appreciate).

On the board, parallel with each edge, are nineteen thin, lacquered black lines. These lines are about four one-hundredths of an inch wide. It has been seen from the dimensions given that the board is not exactly square, and the field therefore is a parallelogram, the sides of which are sixteen and a half and fifteen inches long respectively, and the lines in one direction are a little bit farther apart than in the other. These lines, by their crossing, produce three hundred and sixty-one points of intersection, including the corners and the points along the edge of the field.

The stones are placed on these points of intersection, and not in the spaces as the pieces are in Chess or Checkers. These intersections are called "Me" or "Moku" in Japanese, which really means "an eye." Inasmuch as the word as used in this connection is untranslatable, I shall hereafter refer to these points of intersection by their Japanese name.

On the board, as shown in the diagram (Plate 1), are nine little circles. It is on these circles that the handicap stones when given are placed. They have no other function in the game, but they are supposed also to have some sort of symbolical meaning. Chamberlain states that these spots or "Seimoku" are supposed to represent the chief celestial bodies, and that the central one is called "Taikyoku"; that is, the primordial principle of the universe. In the work of Stewart Culin referred to in the preface it is stated that they correspond to the nine lights of heaven — the sun, moon and the seven stars of the constellation "Tau" (Ursa Major). Indeed the whole arrangement of the board is said to have some symbolical significance, the number of crosses (exclusive of the central one) representing the three hundred and sixty degrees of latitude, and the number of white and black stones corresponding to the number of days of the year; but nowadays the Japanese do not make much of a point of the astronomical significance of the board or of the "Seimoku."

The stones or "Ishi" with which the game is played are three hundred and sixty-one in number, corresponding to the number of "Me" or points of intersection on the board. One hundred and eighty of these stones are white and the remaining one hundred and eighty-one are black. As the weaker player has the black stones and the first move, obviously the extra stone must be black. In practice the entire number of stones is never used, as at the end of the game there are always vacant spaces on the board. The Japanese generally keep these stones in gracefully, shaped, lacquered boxes or "Go tsubo.

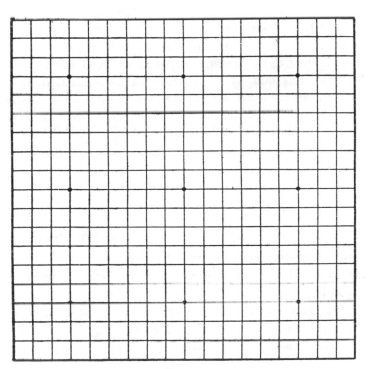

PLATE I

The Board Showing the "Seimoku."

The white stones are made of a kind of white shell; they are highly polished, and are exceedingly pleasant to the touch. The best come from the provinces of Hitachi and Mikawa. The black are made of stone, generally a kind of slate that comes from the Nachi cataract in Kishiu. As they are used they become almost jet-black, and they are also pleasant to the touch, but not so much so as the white. A good set is quite dear, and cannot be purchased under several yen. The ideograph formerly used for "Go ishi" indicates that originally they were made of wood, and not of stone, and the old Chinese ideograph shows that in that country they were wooden pieces painted black and white. The use of polished shell for the white stones was first introduced in the Ashikaga period.

In form the stones are disk-shaped, but not always exactly round, and are convex on both surfaces, so that they tremble slightly when placed on the board. They are about three-quarters of an inch in diameter, and about one-eighth of an inch in thickness. The white stones are generally a trifle larger than the black ones; for some strange reason those of both colors are a little bit wider than they should be in order to fit the board. Korschelt carefully measured the stones which he used, and found that the black were seventeen-sixteenths of the distance between the vertical lines on his board, and about eighteen-nineteenths of the distance between the horizontal lines, while the white stones were thirteen-twelfths of the distance between the vertical lines and thirty-six thirty-sevenths of the distance between the horizontal lines. I found about the same relation of size in the board and stones which I use.

The result of this is that the stones do not have quite room enough and lap over each other, and when the board is very full, they push each other out of place. To make matters still worse the Japanese are not very careful to put the stones exactly on the points of intersection, but place them carelessly, so that the board has an irregular appearance. It is probable that the unsymmetrical shape of the board and the irregularity of the size of the stones arise from the antipathy that the Japanese have to exact symmetry. At any rate, it is all calculated to break up the monotonous appearance which the board would have if the spaces were exactly square, and the stones were exactly round and fitted properly in their places.

In Japan the board is placed on the floor, and the players sit on the floor also, facing each other, as shown in the illustration, and generally the narrower side of the board is placed so as to face the players. Since the introduction of tables in Japan Go boards are also made thinner and without feet, but the game seems to lose some of its charm when the customs of the old Japan are departed from.

The Japanese always take the stone between the middle and index fingers, and not between the thumb and index finger as we are likely to do, and they place it on the board smartly and with great skill, so that it gives a cheerful sound, as before stated.

For use in this country the board need not be so thick, and need not, of course, have feet, but if it is attempted to play the game on cardboard, which has a dead sound as the stones are played, it is surprising how much the pleasure of the game is diminished. The author has found

that Casino chips are the best substitute for the Japanese
stones.

Originally the board used for the game of Go was not
so large, and the intersecting lines in each direction were
only seventeen in number. At the time of the foundation
of the Go Academy this was the size of board in use. As
the game developed the present number of lines became
fixed after trial and comparison with other possible sizes.
Korschelt made certain experiments with the next possible
larger size in which the number of lines in each direction
was twenty-one, and it seemed that the game could still
be played, although it made necessary the intellect of a
past master to grasp the resulting combinations. If more
than twenty-one lines are used Korschelt states that the
combinations are beyond the reach of the human mind.

In closing the description of the board it may be interesting to point out that the game which we call "Go Bang"
or "Five in a Row," is played on what is really a Japanese
Go board, and the word "Go Bang" is merely another
phonetic imitation of the words by which the Japanese
designate their board. I have found, however, that the
"Go Bang" boards sold in the stores in this country are
an imitation of the original Japanese "Go ban," and have
only seventeen lines, and are therefore a little too small
for the game as now played. The game which we call
"Go Bang" also originated in Japan, and is well known
and still played there. They call it "Go Moku Narabe,"
which means to arrange five "Me," the word "Go" in this
case meaning "five," and "Moku" being the alternative
way of pronouncing the ideograph for eye. "Go Moku
Narabe" is often played by good Go players, generally

for relaxation, as it is a vastly simpler game than Go, and can be finished much more rapidly. It is not, however, to be despised, as when played by good players there is considerable chance for analysis, and the play often covers the entire board.

III

RULES OF PLAY

THE players play alternately, and the weaker player has the black stones and plays first, unless a handicap has been given, in which case the player using the white stones has the first move. (In the olden times this was just reversed.) They place the stones on the vacant points of intersection on the board, or "Me," and they may place them wherever they please, with the single exception of the case called "Ko," which will be hereafter explained. When the stones are once played they are never moved again.

The object of the game of Go is to secure territory. Just as the object of the game of Chess is not to capture pieces, but to checkmate the adverse King, so in Go the ultimate object is not to capture the adversary's stones, but to so arrange matters that at the end of the game a player's stones will surround as much vacant space as possible. At the end of the game, however, before the amount of vacant space is calculated, the stones that have been taken are used to fill up the vacant spaces claimed by the adversary; that is to say, the captured black stones are used to fill up the spaces surrounded by the player having the white pieces, and vice versa, and the player who has the greatest amount of territory after the captured stones are used in this way, is the winner of the game. However, if the players, fearing

each other, merely fence in parts of the board without regard to each other's play, a most uninteresting game
results, and the Japanese call this by the contemptuous epithet "Ji dori go," or "ground taking Go." I have noticed
that beginners in this country sometimes start to play in
this way, and it is one of the many ways by which the play
of a mere novice may be recognized. The best games arise
when the players in their efforts to secure territory attack
each other's stones or groups of stones, and we therefore
must know how a stone can be taken.

A stone is taken when it is surrounded on four opposite
sides as shown in Plate 2, Diagram I. When it is taken
it is removed from the board. It is not necessary that a
stone should also be surrounded diagonally, which would
make eight stones necessary in order to take one; neither
do four stones placed on the adjacent diagonal intersections cause a stone to be taken: they do not directly
attack the stone in the center at all. Plate 2, Diagram IV,
shows this situation.

A stone which is placed on the edge of the board may
be surrounded and captured by three stones, as shown in
Plate 2, Diagram II, and if a stone is placed in the extreme
corner of the board, it may be surrounded and taken by
two stones, as shown in Plate 2, Diagram III.

In actual practice it seldom or never happens that a
stone or group of stones is surrounded by the minimum
number requisite under the rule, for in that case the player
whose stones were threatened could generally manage to
break through his adversary's line. It is almost always
necessary to add helping stones to those that are strictly
necessary in completing the capture. Plate 2, Diagram V,

shows four stones which are surrounded with the minimum number of stones. Plate 2, Diagram VI, shows the same group with a couple of helping stones added, which would probably be found necessary in actual play.

It follows from this rule that stones which are on the same line parallel with the edges of the board are connected, and support each other, Plate 2, Diagram VII, while stones which are on the same *diagonal* line are not connected, and do not support each other, Plate 2, Diagram VIII. In order to surround stones which are on the same line, and therefore connected, it is necessary to surround them all in order to take them, while stones which are arranged on a diagonal line, and therefore unconnected, may be taken one at a time. On Plate 2, Diagram III, if there were a stone placed at S 18, it would not be connected with the stone in the corner, and would not help it in any way. On the other hand, as has been said, it is not necessary to place a white stone on that point in order to complete the capture of the stone in the corner.

In order to capture a group or chain of stones containing vacant space, it must be completely surrounded inside and out; for instance, the black group shown on Plate 2, Diagram IX, while it has no hope of life if it is White's play is nevertheless not completely surrounded. In order to surround it, it is necessary to play on the three vacant intersections at M 11, N 11, and O 11. The same group of stones is shown in Diagram X completely surrounded. (It may be said in passing that White must play at N 11 first or the black stones can defend themselves; we shall understand this better in a moment.)

In practice it often happens that a stone or group of

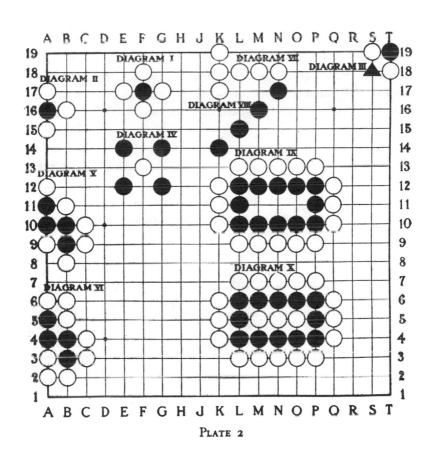

PLATE 2

stones is regarded as dead before it is completely surrounded, because when the situation is observed to be hopeless the losing player abandons it, and addresses his energies to some other part of the board. It is advantageous for the losing player to abandon such a group as soon as possible, for, if he continues to add to the group, he loses not only the territory but the added stones also. If the circumstances are such that his opponent has to reply to his moves in the hopeless territory, the loss is not so great, as the opponent is meanwhile filling up spaces which would otherwise be vacant, and against an inferior player there is a chance of the adversary making a slip and allowing the threatened stones to save themselves. If, however, the situation is so clearly hopeless that the adversary is not replying move for move, then every stone added to such a group means a loss of two points.

At the end of the game such abandoned groups of stones are removed from the board just as if they had been completely surrounded and killed, and it is not necessary for the player having the advantage actually to surround and kill such a group. It is enough if they obviously can be killed. The theory on which this rule proceeds is that if the players play alternately, no advantage would be gained by either side in the process of actually surrounding such a group, and its completion would only be a waste of time. But let us suppose that a black group at the end of the game is found to be hopeless and also completely surrounded with the exception of one point. The question arises, can the Black player demand that his adversary play on the vacant space in order to kill this group, for, if he could, it is obvious he would gain one "Me" by so doing. The answer is, he cannot so demand, and his adversary is not bound to play on this point, and the hopeless or abandoned stones are removed without further play. We might call such groups "dead." They may be distinguished from stones that are "taken," because these latter are removed at once, whereas "dead" stones are removed only at the end of the game.

As a corollary to the rule for surrounding and taking stones, it follows that a group of stones containing two disconnected vacant intersections or "Me" cannot be taken. This is not a separate rule. It follows necessarily from the method by which stones are taken. Nevertheless in practice it is the *most important principle in the game.*

In order to understand the rule or principle of the two "Me," we must first look at the situation shown in Plate 3, Diagram I. There, if a black stone is played at F 15, although it is played on an intersection entirely surrounded by white stones, it nevertheless lives because the moment it is played it has the effect of killing the entire white group; that is to say, a stone may be played on an intersection where it is completely surrounded if as it is played it has the effect of completely surrounding the adversary's stones already on the board. If, on the other hand, we have a situation as shown in Plate 3, Diagram II, a black stone may indeed be played on one of the vacant intersections, but when it is so played the white group is not completely surrounded, because there still remains one space yet to be filled, and the black stone itself is dead as soon as it touches the board, and hence it would be impossible to surround this group of white stones unless two stones were played at once. The white stones, therefore, can never be surrounded, and form an impregnable position.

This is the principle of the two "Me," and when a player's group of stones is hard pressed, and his adversary is trying to surround them, if he can so place the stones that two disconnected complete "Me" are left, they are safe forever. It makes no difference whether the vacant "Me" are on the edges or in the corners of the board, or how far from each other they may be.

Plate 3, Diagram VI, shows a group of stones containing two vacant "Me" on the edge of the board. This group is perfectly safe against attack. A beginner might ask why the white group shown on Plate 3, Diagram V, is not safe. The difficulty with that group is, that when Black has played at S 9, there are no "Me" in it at all as the word is used in this connection, not even a "Kageme" as shown in Plate 3, Diagram III, because a "Me," in order to be available for the purpose of defense, must be a vacant intersection that is surrounded on four sides, just as a captured stone must be surrounded, and therefore on the sides of the board it can be made by three stones, and in the corner of the board by two stones, but it is absolutely necessary, in addition to the minimum number of surrounding stones, to have helping stones to guard the surrounding stones against attack. This brings us to what the Japanese call "Kageme."

In actual play there are many groups of stones that at first glance seem to have two vacant "Me" in them, but which on analysis, will be found vulnerable to attack. A "Me" that looks somewhat as if it were complete, but is, nevertheless, destructible is called "Kageme." "Kage"

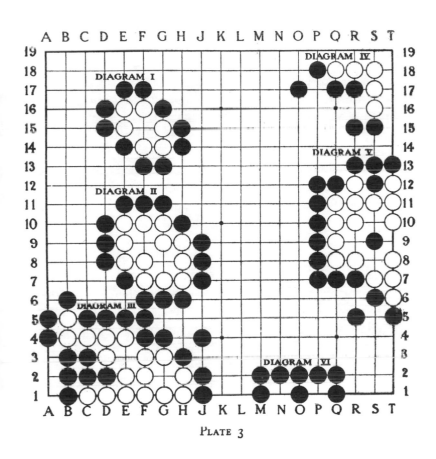

PLATE 3

means "chipped" or "incomplete." Plate 3, Diagram III, is an illustration of this. A beginner might think that the white group was safe, but Black can kill the upper six white stones by playing at E 3, and then on the next move can kill the remainder by playing at G 2. Therefore, E 3 is not a perfect "Me," but is "Kageme." G 2 is a perfect "Me," but one is not enough to save the group. In this group if the stone at F 4 or D 2 were white, there would be two perfect "Me," and the group would be safe. In a close game beginners often find it difficult to distinguish between a perfect "Me" and "Kageme."

Groups of stones which contain vacant spaces, can be lost or saved according as two disconnected "Me" can or cannot be formed in those spaces, and the most interesting play in the game occurs along the sides and especially in the corners of the board in attempting to form or attempting to prevent the formation of these "Me." The attacking player often plays into the vacant space and sacrifices several stones with the ultimate object of reducing the space to one "Me"; and, on the other hand, the defending player by selecting a fortunate intersection may make it impossible for the stones to be killed. There is opportunity for marvelous ingenuity in the attack and defense of these positions. A simple example of defense is shown in Plate 3, Diagram IV, where, if it is White's turn, and he plays in the corner of the board at T 19, he can save his stones. If, on the other hand, he plays anywhere else, the two "Me" can never be formed. The beginner would do well to work out this situation for himself.

The series of diagrams commencing at Plate 3, Diagram V, show the theoretical method of reducing vacant spaces by the sacrifice of stones. This series is taken from Korschelt, and the position as it arose in actual play is shown on Plate 10, depicting a complete game. In Plate 3, Diagram v, the white group is shown externally surrounded, and the black stone has just been played at S 9, rendering the group hopeless. The same group is shown on the opposite side of the board at Plate 4, Diagram I, but Black has added three more stones and could kill the white gro up on the next move. Therefore, White plays at A 12, and the situation shown in Plate 4, Diagram II, arises, where the same group is shown on the lower edge of the board. Now, if it were White's move, he could save his group by playing at J 2, and the situation which would then arise is shown on Plate 4, Diagram III, where White has three perfect "Me," one more than enough. However, it is not White's move, and Black plays on the coveted intersection, and then adds two more stones until the situation shown in Plate 4, Diagram IV, arises. Then White must again play at S 8 in order to save his stones from immediate capture, and the situation shown at Plate 5, Diagram I, comes about. Black again plays at J 18, adds one more stone, and we have the situation shown in Plate 5, Diagram II, where it is obvious that White must play at C 11 in order to save his group from immediate capture, thus leaving only two vacant spaces. It is unnecessary to continue the analysis further, but at the risk of explaining what is apparent, it might be pointed out that Black would play on one of these vacant spaces, and if White killed the stone (which it would not pay White to do) Black would play again on the space thus made vacant, and completely surround and kill the entire white group.

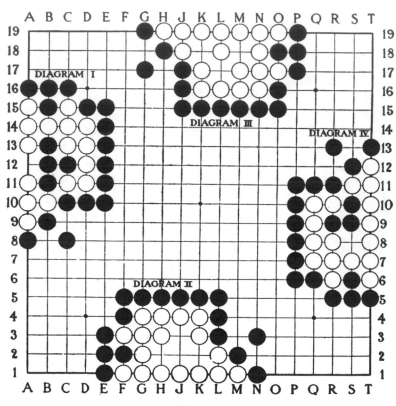

PLATE 4

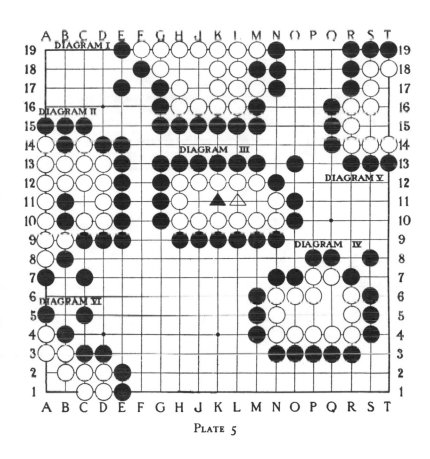

PLATE 5

A group with five vacant "Me," as shown in the pre-ceding diagrams, is a situation well known to the Japanese, so much so that they have a special phrase or saying that applies to it, to wit, "Go moku naka de wa ju san te," which means that it takes thirteen turns to reduce a group having five such "Me" in the center.

As we have previously seen, in actual play this white group would be regarded as "dead" as distinguished from "taken," and this series of moves would not be played out. White obviously would not play in the space, and he could not demand that Black play therein in order to complete the actual surrounding of the stones, and the only purpose of giving this series of diagrams is to show theoretically how the white stones can be killed. However, the killing of these stones would be necessary if the surrounding black line were in turn attacked ("Semeai"), in which case it might be a race to see whether the internal white stones could be completely surrounded and killed before the external white group could get in complete contact with the black line.

Stones which are sacrificed in order to kill a larger group are called "Sute ishi" by the Japanese, from "Suteru," meaning "to cast or throw away," and "Ishi," a "stone."

It may be noted that if a group contains four connected vacant intersections in a line it is safe, because if the adversary attempts to reduce it, two disconnected "Me" can be formed in the space by simply playing a stone adjacent to the adversary's stone, as shown in Plate 5, Diagram III, where, if Black plays for instance at K 11, White replies at L 11, and secures the two "Me." Even if these four connected vacant intersections are not in a straight line, they

are nevertheless sufficient for the purpose, provided the
fourth "Me" is connected at the end of the three, and the
Japanese express this by their saying "Magari shimoku wa
me," or four "Me" turning a corner. Neither does it make
any difference whether the four connected "Me" are in the
center of the board or along the edge. On Plate 5, Diagrams
IV and V, are examples of "Magari shimoku wa me," and
they both are safe. It is interesting, however, to compare
these situations with that shown at Plate 4, Diagram II,
where the fourth intersection is not connected at the end of
the line, and which group Black can kill if it is his move,
as we already have seen.

If, however, such a group contains only three connected
vacant intersections, and it is the adversary's move, it can
be killed, because the adversary by playing on the middle
intersection can prevent the formation of two disconnected
"Me." We saw a group of this kind on Plate 2, Diagram
IX, which can be killed by playing at N 11. Obviously, if
it is Black's move in this case, the group can be saved by
playing at N 11; obviously, also, if White, being a mere
novice, plays elsewhere than at N 11, Black saves the stones
by playing there and killing the white stone. Plate 5,
Diagram VI, shows another group containing only three
vacant intersections. These can be killed if it is Black's
move by playing at A 1. On the other hand, if it is White's
move, he can save them by playing on the same point.

Of course, if a group of stones contains a large number
of vacant intersections, it is perfectly safe unless the vacant
space is so large that the adversary can have a chance of
forming an entire new living group of stones therein.

We now come to the one exception to the rule that the

players may place their stones at will on any vacant intersection on the board. This rule is called the rule of "Ko,"
and is shown on Plate 6, Diagram I. Assuming that it is
White's turn to play, he can play at D 17 and take the black
stone at C 17 which is already surrounded on three sides,
and the position shown in Plate 6, Diagram II, would then
arise. It is now Black's turn to play, and if he plays at C 13,
the white stone which has just been put down will be like-
wise surrounded and could be at once taken from the board.
Black, however, is not permitted to do this immediately,
but must first play somewhere else, and this gives White
the choice of filling up this space (C 13) and defending his
stone, or of following his adversary to some other portion of
the board. The reason for this rule in regard to "Ko" is
very clear. If the players were permitted to take and retake the stones as shown in the diagram, the series of moves
would be endless, and the game could never be finished.
It is something like perpetual check in Chess, but the Japanese, in place of calling the game a draw, compel the second
player to move elsewhere and thus allow the game to continue. In an actual game when a player is prevented from
retaking a stone by the rule of "Ko," he always tries to play
in some other portion of the board where he threatens a
larger group of stones than is involved in the situation where
"Ko" occurs, and thus often he can compel his adversary
to follow him to this other part of the field, and then return
to retake in "Ko." His adversary then will play in some
part of the field, if possible, where another group can be
threatened, and so on. Sometimes in a hotly contested
game the battle will rage around a place where "Ko" occurs
and the space will be taken and retaken several times.

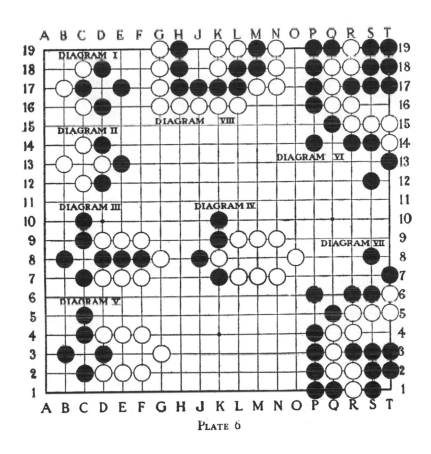

PLATE 6

Korschelt states that the ideograph for "Ko" means "talent" or "skilfulness," in which he is very likely wrong, as it is more accurately translated by our word "threat"; but be this as it may, it is certainly true that the rule in regard to "Ko" gives opportunity for a great display of skill, and as the better players take advantage of this rule with much greater ingen; ;y, it is a good idea for the weaker player as far as possible to avoid situations where its application arises.

There is a situation which sometimes arises and which might be mistaken for "Ko." It is where a player takes more than one stone and the attacking stone is threatened on three sides, or where only one stone is taken, but the adversary in replying can take not only the last stone played, but others also. In these cases the opponent can retake immediately, because it will at once be seen that an endless exchange of moves (which makes necessary the rule of "Ko") would not occur. A situation of this kind is shown on Plate 6, Diagrams iii, iv, and v, where White by playing at C 8 (Diagram iii) takes the three black stones, producing the situation shown in Diagram iv, and Black is permitted immediately to retake the white stone, producing the state of affairs shown in Diagram v. The Japanese call such a situation "Ute kaeshi," which means "returning a blow." It forms no exception to the ordinary rules of the game, and only needs to be pointed out because a beginner might think that the rule of "Ko" applied to it.

We will now take up the situation called "Seki." "Seki" means a "barrier" or "impasse" — it is a different word from the "Seki" in the phrase "Jo seki." "Seki" also is somewhat analagous to perpetual check. It arises when a vacant space is surrounded partly by white and partly by black stones in such a way that, if either player places a stone therein, his adversary can thereupon capture the entire group. Under these circumstances, of course, neither player desires to place a stone on that portion of the board, and the rules of the game do not compel him to do so. That portion of the board is regarded as neutral territory, and at the end of the game the vacant "Me" are not counted in favor of either player. Plate 6, Diagram VI, gives an illustration of "Seki," where it will be seen that if Black plays at either S 16 or T 16 White can kill the black stones in the corner by playing on the other point, and if White plays on either point Black can kill the white stones by filling the remaining vacancy. Directly below, on Diagram VII, is shown the same group, but the corner black stone has been taken out. The position is now no longer "Seki," but is called by the Japanese "Me ari me nashi," or literally "having 'Me,' not having 'Me.' " Here the white stones are dead, because if Black plays, for instance, at T 4 White cannot kill the black stones by playing at S 4, for the reason that the vacant "Me" at T 1 still remains. The beginner might confuse "Seki" with "Me ari me nashi," and while a good player has no trouble in recognizing the difference when the situation arises, it takes considerable foresight sometimes so to play as to produce one situation or the other.

Plate 6, Diagram VIII, shows another group which might be mistaken for "Seki," but here, if White plays at J 19, the black stones can be killed, further proceedings being somewhat similar to those we saw in the illustration of "Go moku naka de wa ju san te." Plate 7 shows a large group of stones from which inevitably "Seki" will result. It would be well for the student to work this out for himself. "Seki" very seldom or never occurs in games between good players, and it rarely occurs in any game.

It is a rule of the game to give warning when a stone or group of stones is about to be completely surrounded. For this purpose the Japanese use the word "Atari" (from "ataru," to touch lightly), which corresponds quite closely to the expression "gardez" in Chess. If this warning were omitted, the player whose stones were about to be taken should have the right to take his last move over and save the imperiled position if he could. This rule is not so strictly observed as formerly; it belongs more to the etiquette of the old Japan.

The game comes to an end when the frontiers of the opposing groups are in contact. This does not mean that the board is entirely covered, for the obvious reason that the space inside the groups or chains of stones is purposely left vacant, for that is the only part of the board which counts; but so long as there is any vacant space lying *between* the opposing groups that must be disposed of in some way, and when it is so disposed of it will be found that the white and black groups are in complete contact.

Just at the end of the game there will be found isolated vacant intersections or "Me" on the frontier lines, and it does not make any difference which player fills these up. They are called by the Japanese "Dame," which means "useless." (The word "Dame" is likely to be confusing when it is first heard, because the beginner jumps to the conclusion that it is some new kind of a "Me." This arises from a coincidence only. Anything that is useless or profit-

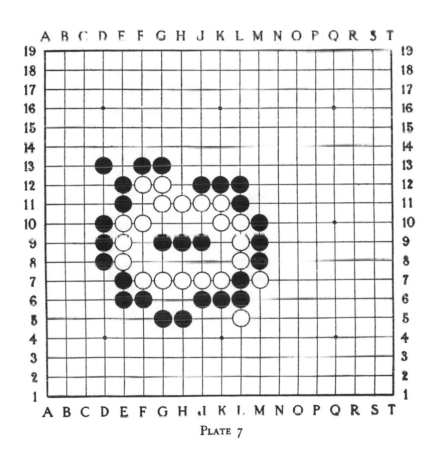

PLATE 7

less is called "Dame" in Japanese, but etymologically the word really means "horse's eye," as the Japanese, not being admirers of the vacant stare of that noble animal, have used this word as a synonym for all that is useless. Therefore the syllable "Me" does mean an eye, and is the same word that is used to designate the intersections, but its recurrence in this connection is merely an accident.)

It is difficult for the beginner at first to understand why the filling of these "Dame" results in no advantage to either player, and beginners often fill up such spaces even before the end of the game, feeling that they are gaining ground slowly but surely; and the Japanese have a saying, "Heta go ni dame nashi," which means that there are no "Dame" in beginners' Go, as beginners do not recognize their use-lessness. On the other hand, a necessary move will some-times look like "Dame." The moves that are likely to be so confused are the final connecting moves or "Tsugu," where a potential connection has been made early in the game, but which need to be filled up to complete the chain. In the Illustrative Game, Number 1, the "Dame" are all given, but a little practice is necessary before they can always be recognized.

When the "Dame" have been filled, and the dead stones have been removed from the board, there is no reason why the players should not at once proceed to counting up which of them has the greatest amount of vacant space, less, of course, the number of stones they have lost, and thus deter-mine who is the victor. As a matter of practice, however, the Japanese do not do this immediately, but, purely for the purpose of facilitating the count, the player having the white pieces would fill up his adversary's territory with the black stones he had captured as far as they would go, and the player having the black stones would fill up his adversary's territory with the white stones that he had captured; and thereupon the entire board is reconstructed, so that the vacant spaces come into rows of fives and tens, so that they are easier to count. This has really nothing to do with the game, and it is merely a device to make the counting of the spaces easier, but it seems like a mysterious process to a novice, and adds not a little to the general mystery with which the end of the game seems to be surrounded when an Occidental sees it played for the first time. This process of arrangement is called "Me wo tsukuru." It may be added that if any part of the board contains the situation called "Seki," that portion is left alone, and is not reconstructed like the rest of the board.

Plate 8 shows a completed game in which the "Dame" have all been filled, but the dead stones have not yet been removed from the board. Let us first see which of the stones are dead. It is easy to see that the white stone at N 11 is hopeless, as it is cut off in every direction. The same is true of the white stone at B 18. It is not so easy to see that the black stones at L and M 18, N, O, P, Q and R 17, N 16, and M and N 15 are dead, but against a good player they would have no hope of forming the necessary two "Me," and they are therefore conceded to be dead; but a good player could probably manage to defend them against a novice. It is still more difficult to see why the irregular white group of eighteen stones on the left-hand side of the board has been abandoned, but there also White has no chance of making the necessary two "Me." At the risk of repetition I will again point out that these groups of dead stones can be taken from the board without further play.

Plate 9 shows the same game after the dead stones have been removed and used to fill up the respective territories, and after the board has been reconstructed in accordance with the Japanese method, and it will be seen that in this case Black has won by one stone. This result can be arrived at equally well by counting up the spaces on Plate 8, but they are easier to count on Plate 9, after the "Me wo tsukuru" has been done.

Plate 10 shows another completed game. This plate is from Korschelt, and is interesting because it contains an instructive error. The game is supposed to be completed, and the black stone at C 18 is said to be dead. This is not true, because Black by playing at C 17 could not only save his stone, but kill the four white stones at the left-hand side. Therefore, before this game is completed, White must play at C 17 to defend himself. This is called "Tsugu." On the left-hand side of the board is shown a white group which is dead, and the method of reduction of which we have already studied in detail. On the right side of the board are a few scattering black stones which are dead, because they have no chance of forming a group with the necessary two "Me." The question may be asked whether it is necessary for White to play at C 1 or E 1 in order to complete the connection of the group in the corner, but he is not obliged so to do unless Black chooses to play at B 1 or F 1, which, of course, Black would not do.

On Plate 11, this game also is shown as reconstructed for counting, and it will be seen that White has won by two stones. Really this is an error of one stone, as White

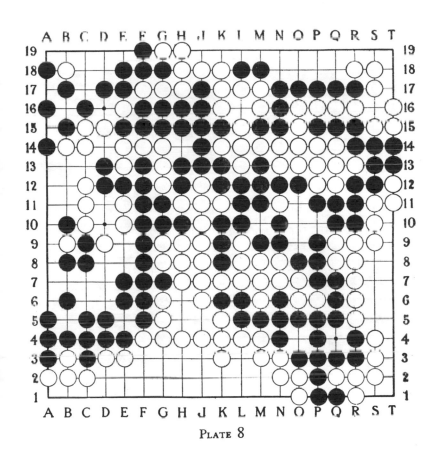

PLATE 8

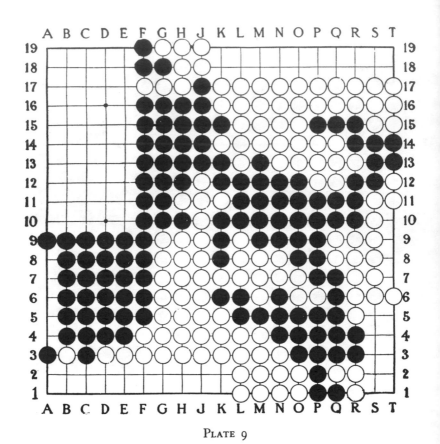

PLATE 9

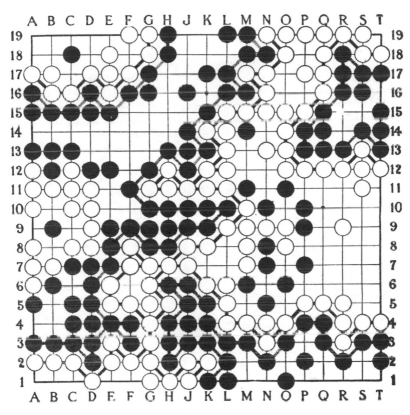

PLATE 10

should have played at C 17, as we have previously pointed
out.

Sometimes at the end of the game players of moder-
ate skill may differ as to whether there is anything left to
be done, and when one thinks there is no longer any advantage to be gained by either side, he says, "Mo arimasen, aru
naraba o yuki nasai," that is to say, "I think there is nothing
more to be done; if you think you can gain anything, you
may play," and sometimes he will allow his adversary to play
two or three times in succession, reserving the right to step
in if he thinks there is a chance of his adversary reviving
a group that is apparently dead.

No part of the rules of the game has been more difficult
for me to understand than the methods employed at the end,
and especially the rule in regard to the removal of dead
stones without actually surrounding them, but I trust in
the foregoing examples I have made this rule sufficiently
clear.   Moreover, it is not always easy to tell whether stones
are dead or alive.   There is a little poem or "Hokku" in
Japanese, which runs as follows:

> "Iki shini wo
> Shiranu nonki no
> Go uchi kana,"

which might be translated as "Oh! what kind of a Go
player is he who does not know whether his stones are alive
or dead!"   But while the Japanese author of this "Hokku"
may have regarded it as a simple thing, the Occidental student of the game would not be likely to share his views.
An instance of this is shown by the possibilities of the sup-
posedly dead black stone on Plate 10, and I think it would
be fairer to state that the skill of a good Go player is most

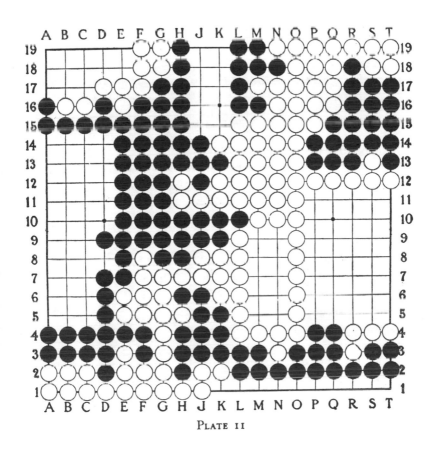

PLATE 11

clearly shown by his ability to recognize immediately whether a group is dead or can be saved; the study of our chapter on Problems will give further illustrations of the difficulty and nicety of such decisions.

We now come to the question of handicaps. Handicaps are given by the stronger player allowing the weaker player to place a certain number of stones on the board before the game begins, and we have seen in the chapter on the Description of the Board that these stones are placed on the nine dotted intersections. If one stone is given, it is usual to place it in the upper right-hand corner. If a second stone is given, it is placed in the lower left-hand corner. If a third stone is given, it is placed in the lower right-hand corner. The fourth is placed in the upper left-hand corner. The fifth is placed at the center or "Ten gen." When six are given, the center one is removed, and the fifth and sixth are placed at the left and right-hand edges of the board on line 10. If seven are given, these stones remain, and the seventh stone is placed in the center. If eight are given, the center stone is again removed, and the seventh and eighth stones are placed on the "Seimoku" on line K. If the ninth is given, it is again placed in the center of the board.

Between players of reasonable skill more than nine stones are never given, but when the disparity between the players is too great, four other stones are sometimes given. They are placed just outside the corner "Seimoku," as shown on the diagram (Plate 12), and these extra stones are called "Furin" handicaps. "Furin" means "a small bell," as these stones suggest to the Japanese the bells which hang from the eaves at the corners of a Japanese temple. When the disparity between the players is very great indeed, some-

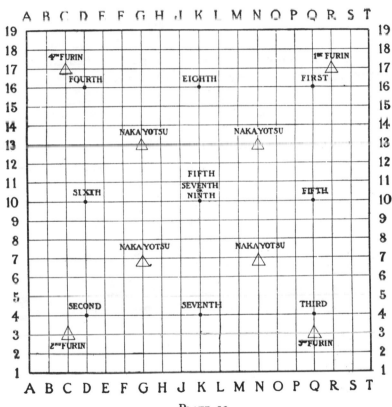

PLATE 12

times four more stones are given, and when given they are placed on the diagonal half way between the corner "Seimo-ku" and the center. These four stones are called "Naka yotsu," or "the four middle stones," but such a handicap could only be given to the merest novice.

We have now completed a survey of all the actual rules of the game, and it may be well to summarize them in order that their real simplicity may be clearly seen; briefly, they are as follows:

1. The object of the game is to obtain vacant territory.

2. The stones are placed on the intersections and on any vacant intersection the player chooses (except in the case of "Ko"). After they are played they are not moved again.

3. (a) One or more stones which are compactly surrounded by the stones of the other side are said to be taken and are at once removed from the board.

(b) Stones which, while not actually surrounded can inevitably be surrounded, are dead, and can be taken from the board at the end of the game without further play.

(c) Taken or dead stones are used to fill up the adversary's territory.

4. The game is at an end when the opposing groups of stones are in absolute contact (the case of "Seki" being the single exception).

It is not possible to imagine a game with simpler rules, or the elements of which are easier to acquire.

We will now turn our attention to a few considerations as to the best methods of play, and of certain moves and formations which occur in every game, and also to the names which in Japanese are used to designate these things.

GENERAL METHODS OF PLAY AND TERMINOLOGY OF THE GAME

As will be shown more in detail in the chapter on Openings or " Joseki," the game is commenced by playing in the corners of the board, and generally on one of the squares adjacent to the handicap point. The reason for this is that the corners of the board are natural fortresses, and can be more readily defended against attack. It is also easier to form territory in the corners of the board. Next to the corners of the board the sides of the board are easiest to defend, and territory is more easily formed along the sides than in the center, and in an ordinary game the play generally proceeds from the corners and edges to the center. The importance which the Japanese attach to the corners is shown by their saying "Yo sumi torarete go wo utsu na," or, "if the four corners are taken, cease playing." Against a good player it is next to impossible to form territory in the center of the board, unless it is based on one of the sides or corners.

There is, however, an old rule of etiquette which is not consistent with this theory of the opening; it used to be regarded as exceedingly impolite and insulting to play the first stone on the handicap point in the center of the board, called "Ten gen." It has been explained to me that the reason for this rule is that such a move was supposed to

assure the victory to the first player, and it is related that
when on one occasion Murase Shuho had defeated a rival
many times in succession, the latter, becoming desperate, apol-
ogized for his rudeness and placed his stone on this spot, and
Murase, nevertheless, succeeded in winning the game, which
was regarded as evidence of his great skill.   It has, however,
been shown by Honinbo Dosaku that this move gives the
first player no decisive advantage, and I have been also told
by some Japanese that the reason that this move is regarded
as impolite is because it is a wasted move, and implies a
disrespect for the adversary's skill, and from what experi-
ence I have had in the game I think the latter explanation
is more plausible.   At all events, such a move is most un-
usual and can only be utilized by a player of the highest
skill.

When good players commence the game, from the first
they have in mind the entire board, and they generally play
a stone in each of the four corners and one or two around
the edges of the board, sketching out, as it were, the territory which they ultimately hope to obtain.   They do not
at once attack each other's stones, and it is not until the
game is well advanced that anything like a hand to hand
conflict occurs.   Beginners are likely to engage at once in
a close conflict.   Their minds seem to be occupied with an
intense desire to surround and capture the first stones the
adversary places on the board, and often their opposing
groups of stones, starting in one corner, will spread out in
a struggling mass from that point all over the board.   There
is no surer indication of the play of a novice than this.   It
is just as if a battle were to commence without the guidance
of a commanding officer, by indiscriminate fisticuffs among

the common soldiers. Of the other extreme, or "Ji dori Go," we have already spoken. Another way in which the play of experts may be recognized is that all the stones of a good player are likely to be connected in one or at most two groups, while poorer players find their stones divided up into small groups each of which has to struggle to form the necessary two "Me" in order to insure survival.

Assuming that we have advanced far enough to avoid premature encounters or "Ji dori Go," and are placing our stones in advantageous positions, decently and in order, the question arises, how many spaces can be safely skipped from stone to stone in advancing our frontiers; that is to say, how far can stones be separated and yet be potentially connected, and therefore safe against attack? The answer is, that two spaces can safely be left if there are no adversary's stones in the immediate vicinity. To demonstrate this, let us suppose that Black has stones at R 13 and R 16, and White tries to cut them off from each other. White's best line of attack would be as follows:

White	Black
R 14	S 14
R 15	S 15
Q 16	R 17
Q 13	R 12
Q 12	

and Black has made good his connection, or Black at his fourth move could play at Q 14, then

W	B
Q 15	R 12
P 14 takes.	

There are other continuations, but they are still worse for White. If, however, the adversary's stones are already posted on the line of advance sometimes it is only safe to skip one point, and of course in close positions the stones must be played so that they are actually connected. The Japanese call this skipping of "Me" by the terms "Ikken tobi," "Nikken tobi," "Sangen tobi," etc., which literally means "to fly one, two, or three spaces." Although this is plain enough, these relations are nevertheless shown on Plate 13, Diagrams I, II, and III. When stones of opposite colors on the same line are separated by vacant space in a similar way (Diagram IV), then the terms "Ikken kakari," "Nikken kakari," etc., are used. "Kakari" really means "to hang" or "to be related," but as used in this sense it might be translated "to attack."

Sometimes the stones are placed in relation to each other like the Knight's move in Chess. The Knight in Japanese is called "Keima," or "the honorable horse," and if the stones are of the same color the relation is called "Keima" or "Kogeima," "Ko" being the diminutive. If the stones are of opposite colors, then the phrase "Keima" or "Kogeima kakari" is used as in the previous case. The Japanese also designate a relation similar to the Knight's move, but farther apart, by special words; thus, if the stones are one space farther apart, it is called "Ogeima," or "the Great Knight's move," and if the stone is advanced one step still farther, it is called "Daidaigeima," or "the Great Great Knight's move." On Plate 13, Diagrams V, VI, and VII, are shown "Kogeima," "Ogeima," and "Daidaigeima."

The next question that will trouble the beginner is where to place his stones when his adversary is advancing into his

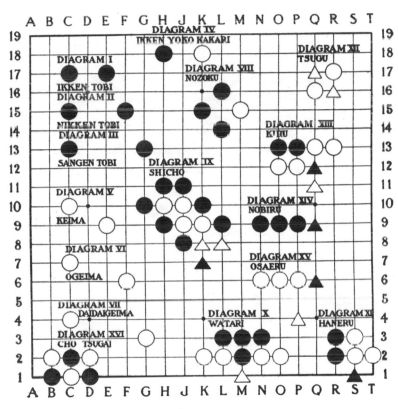

PLATE 13

territory, and beginners are likely to play their stones directly in contact with the advancing forces. This merely results in their being engulfed by the attacking line, and the stones and territory are both lost. If you wish to stop your adversary's advance, play your stones a space or two apart from his, so that you have a chance to strengthen your line before his attack is upon you.

The next thing we will speak of is what the Japanese call the "Sente." This word means literally "the leading hand," but is best translated by our words "having the offensive." It corresponds quite closely to the word "attack," as it is used in Chess, but in describing a game of Go it is better to reserve the word "attack" for a stronger demonstration than is indicated by the word "Sente." The "Sente" merely means that the player having it can compel his adversary to answer his moves or else sustain worse damage, and sometimes one player will have the "Sente" in one portion of the board, and his adversary may disregard the attack and by playing in some other quarter take the "Sente" there. Sometimes the defending player by his ingenious moves may turn the tables on his adversary and wrest the "Sente" from him. At all events, holding the "Sente" is an advantage, and the annotations on illustrative games abound with references to it, and conservative authors on the game advise abandoning a stone or two for the purpose of taking the "Sente."

Sometimes a player has three stones surrounding a vacant space, as shown in Plate 13, Diagram VIII, and the question arises how to attack this group. This is done by playing on the fourth intersection. The Japanese call this "Nozoku," or "peeping into," and when a stone is played

in this way it generally forces the adversary to fill up that
"Me." It may be mentioned here also that when your
adversary is trying to form "Me" in a disputed territory,
the way to circumvent him is to play your stones on one of
the four points he will obviously need to complete his "Me,"
and sometimes this is done before he has three of the necessary stones on the board. The term "Nozoku" is also
applied to any stone which is played as a preliminary move
in cutting the connection between two of the adversary's
stones or groups of stones.

Sometimes a situation occurs as shown in Plate 13,
Diagram IX. Here it is supposed to be White's move, and
he must, of course, play at K 8, whereupon Black would
play at K 7 ("Osaeru"), and White would have to play at
L 8 ("Nobiru"), and so on until, if these moves were per-
sisted in, the formation would stretch in a zigzag line to
the edge of the board. This situation is called "Shicho,"
which really means "a running attack." It results in the
capture of the white stones when the edge of the board is
reached, unless they happen to find a comrade posted on
the line of retreat, for instance, at P 4, in which case they
can be saved. Of course, between good players "Shicho"
is never played out to the end, for they can at once see
whether or not the stones will live, and often a stone placed
seemingly at random in a distant part of the board is played
partly with the object of supporting a retreating line should
"Shicho" occur.

Plate 13, Diagram x, shows a situation that often arises,
in which the White player, by putting his stone at M 1 on
the edge of the board, can join his two groups of stones.
This is so because if Black plays at L 1 or N 1, White can

immediately kill the stone. This joining on the edge of the board is called by the special term "Watari," which means "to cross over." Sometimes we find the word "Watari" used when the connection between two groups is made in a similar way, although not at the extreme edge of the board.

A much more frequent situation is shown at Plate 13, Diagram XI. It is not worthy of special notice except because a special word is applied to it. If Black plays at S 1, it is called "Haneru," which really means the flourish which is made in finishing an ideograph.

We will now take up a few of the other words that are used by the Japanese as they play the game. By far the most frequent of these are "Tsugu," "Kiru," "Nobiru," and "Osaeru." "Tsugu" means "to connect," and when two stones are adjacent but on the diagonal, as shown in Plate 13, Diagram XII, it is necessary to connect them if an attack is threatened. This may be done by playing on either side; that is to say, at Q 17 or R 16. If, on the other hand, Black should play on both these points, the white stones would be forever separated, and this cutting off is called "Kiru," although, as a rule, when such a situation is worthy of comment, one of the intersections has already been filled by the attacking player. Plate 13, Diagram XIII, illustrates "Kiru," where, if a black stone is played at Q 12, the white stones are separated. "Kiru" means "to cut," and is recognizable as one of the component parts of that much abused and mispronounced word "Harakiri." "Nobiru" means "to extend," and when there is a line of stones it means the adding of another one at the end, not skipping a space as in the case of "Ikken tobi," but extending with the stones absolutely connected. In Plate 13, Diagram xiv, if Black plays at Q 9 it would be called "Nobiru." "Osaeru" means "to press down," and this is what we do when we desire to prevent our adversary from extending his line, as seen in the preceding diagram. It is done by playing directly at the end of the adversary's line, as shown in Diagram xv, where Black is supposed to play at Q 6. Here White must play on one side of the black stone, but it must be pointed out that unless there is support in the neighborhood for the stone used in "Osaeru," the stone thus played runs the risk of capture. In Diagram ix, explaining "Shicho," we also had an illustration of "Nobiru" and "Osaeru."

If a stone is played on the intersection diagonally adjacent to another stone, it is called "Kosumu," but this word is not nearly so much used as the other four. Sometimes, also, when it is necessary to connect two groups of stones instead of placing the stone so as actually to connect them, as in the case of "Tsugu," the stone is played so as to effectively guard the point of connection and thus prevent the adversary's stone from separating the two groups. This play is called "Kake tsugu," or "a hanging connection"; e.g., in Diagram xiii, if a white stone were played at Q 11 it would be an instance of "Kake tsugu" and would have prevented the black stone from cutting off the White connection at Q 12, for, if the black stone were played there after a white stone had been placed at Q 11, White could capture it on the next move.

Passing from these words which describe the commonest moves in the game, we will mention the expression "Te okure" — literally "a slow hand" or "a slow move," which means an unnecessary or wasted move. Many of the moves of a beginner are of this character, especially when he has a territory pretty well fenced in and cannot make up his mind whether or not it is necessary to strengthen the group before proceeding to another field of battle. In annotating the best games, also, it is used to mean a move that is not the best possible move, and we frequently hear it used by Japanese in criticising the play.

"Semeai" is another word with which we must be familiar. It means "mutually attacking," from "Semeru," "to attack," and "Au," "to encounter," that is to say, if the White player attacks a group of black stones, the Black player answers by endeavoring to surround the surrounding stones, and so on. In our Illustrative Game, Number 1, the play in the upper right-hand corner of the board is an example of "Semeai." It is in positions of this kind that the condition of affairs called "Seki" often comes about.

Plate 13, Diagram XVI, shows a position which is illustrated only because a special name is applied to it. The Japanese call such a relation of stones "Cho tsugai," literally, "the hinge of a door."

The last expression which we will give is "Naka oshi gatchi," which is the term applied to a victory by a large margin in the early part of the game. These Japanese words mean "to conquer by pushing the center." Beginners are generally desirous of achieving a victory in this way, and are not content to allow their adversary any portion of the board. It is one of the first things to be remembered, that, no matter how skilful a player may be, his adversary will always be able to acquire some territory, and one of the maxims of the game is not to attempt to achieve too great a victory.

Before proceeding with the technical chapters on the Illustrative Games, Openings, etc., it may be well to say a word in regard to the method adopted for keeping a record of the game. The Japanese do this by simply showing a picture of the finished game, on which each stone is numbered as it was played. If a stone is taken and another stone is put in its place, an annotation is made over the diagram of the board with a reference to that intersection, stating that such a stone has been taken in "Ko." Such a method with the necessary marginal annotation is good enough, but it is very hard to follow, as there is no means of telling where any stone is without searching all over the board for it; and while the Japanese are very clever at this, Occidental students of the game do not find it so easy. Therefore, I have adopted the method suggested by Korschelt, which in turn is founded on the custom of Chess annotation in use all over the world. The lines at the bottom of the board are lettered from A to T, the letter I being omitted, and at the sides of the board they are numbered up from 1 to 19. Thus it is always easy to locate any given stone. In the last few years the Japanese have commenced to adopt an analogous method of notation.

V

ILLUSTRATIVE GAMES
I

Plate 14

WHITE. — Iwasa Kei, fifth degree.
BLACK. — Madame Tsutsuki Yoneko, second degree.
Black has a handicap of two stones.
Played about October, 1906. The record is from the
"Tokio Nichi Nichi."

This game is selected because it is very thoroughly
played out. The notes are intended for beginners, and
much is stated which is obvious to a player of any skill;
supplementing the explanations made in the preceding
chapter the Japanese names of the various moves are given.

WHITE	BLACK
1. C 15. A rather unusual move called "Moku hadzushi." As will be seen in the chapter on "Joseki," it is the least conservative of the three usual openings.	**2.** R 4. Called "Komoku," the most usual and most conservative method of commencing the corner play.
3. P 3.	**4.** Q 5. Intended to attack No. 3, and also it commences to make territory on the right side of the board.
5. D 17. This move secures this corner for White.	**6.** O 4. Continues the attack on No. 3.
7. N 3. ("Ikken tobi") M 3 would be too far.	**8.** R 10. Black tries to make territory on the right side.

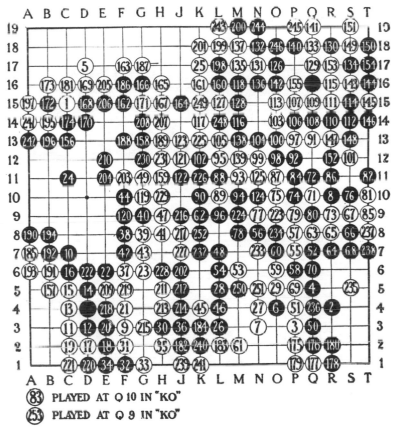

83 PLAYED AT Q 10 IN "KO"

253 PLAYED AT Q 9 IN "KO"

PLATE 14

9. F 3. ("Kogeima.") This is the usual move.

11. C 3.

13. C 4. ("Nobiru.") Giving aid to No. 11.

15. C 5.

17. D 2.

19. C 2. ("Tsugu.") This move is necessary.

21. F 4. Supporting No. 9. "Ikken tobi" would be dangerous.

23. G 6.

25. K 17. Aiming to make territory at the top of the board.

27. N 4. This is necessary to lead out the stone at N 3. "Ikken tobi" would be dangerous.

29. O 5.

10. C 7. ("Ogeima.") This is the usual reply. See the chapter on "Joseki."

12. D 3. Cutting off No. 11.

14. D 5.

16. C 6. ("Osaeru.") Black could not do this before.

18. E 2.

20. E 3. ("Tsugu.") White now has the corner, but Black has possibilities of expansion.

22. E 6. Connecting and at the same time attacking White.

24. C 11. Making territory on the left side of the board.

26. L 3. Precipitate.

Comment by Honinbo Shuye : "Black's twenty-sixth move is premature, and it has the effect of precipitating the contest too early in the game. The territory around that point is dangerous ground for Black. N 17 would have been better."

28. L 5. Leading out toward the center. ("Ikken taka tobi.")

Comment by Honinbo Shuye : "Black should have played at H 4. White would then play at F 2, and Black would reply at E 1."

30. H 3. Taking territory.

Comment by Honinbo Shuye : "Black should still play at H 4."

WHITE

31. F 2. Preventing the connection of the two Black groups.

    33. G 1.

35. H 2. Protecting the connection at G 2.

    37. F 6.

39. G 8. This move prevents White from being shut in.

    41. H 8. ("Nobiru.")

    43. G 7. Necessary to connect.

45. K 4. White threatens to break through in two places.

    47. H 9.

49. G 11. This connects White's groups and prevents Black from extending.

    51. P 4.

53. M 6. This move gives White the "Sente."

55. P 7. Leading out the small White group.

BLACK

32. F 1. ("Haneru.")

34. E 1. ("Tsugu.") This series of moves is necessary and often occurs in the game.

36. J 3. Black must connect, otherwise the stone at H 3 is lost.

38. F 8. Aiming to make territory.

    Comment by Honinbo Shuye: "This move does not hit the spot. It should have been played at L 7."

40. G 9.

42. F 7. Black completes his frontier.

44. F 10. This secures the connection at F 9, and at the same time extends.

46. L 4.

48. L 7. Leading out the stones on line L, which are now threatened.

50. Q 3.

52. Q 7. Making territory on the right and at the same time attacking White's five stones.

54. L 6. Black must connect.

56. N 8. A dangerous move.

Comment by Honinbo Shuye : "This move may be called a little dangerous. P 6 would have been preferable, and if White responds at O 8 or O 7, Black could reply at L 9."

57. P 8.

58. P 6.

59. O 6.

60. O 7. ("Kiru.") Cutting off connection of the white groups.

61. M 2. Since White is cut off at O 7, he must form "Me" in this group.

62. K 9. Black sees that White can form the necessary two "Me," and therefore does not press the attack.

63. Q 8.

64. R 7. Black must extend in this way.

65. R 8.

66. S 8. ("Osaeru.")

67. S 9.

68. S 7. ("Tsugu.") The usual series of moves.

69. P 5. ("Atari.")

70. Q 6.

71. Q 10.

72. Q 11

73. R 9.

74. P 10. ("Sente.")

75. O 10. White must sacrifice No. 71 in order to escape.

76. S 10.

77. N 9.

78. M 8.

79. P 9.

80. Q 9. Takes. This is "Ko."

81. T 10. ("Haneru.")

82. T 11. ("Osaeru.")

83. Q 10. Taking in "Ko."

84. P 11. ("Tsugu.") Black must play here to save the frontier.

85. T 9. Saving the stone at T 10.

86. R 11. Black cannot neglect to play here.

87. O 11.

88. L 11.

89. L 10.

90. K 10.

91. Q 13. White must break up Black's territory in the upper right-hand corner.

92. P 12.

93. M 11. White retreats.

94. M 10.

WHITE	BLACK
95. L 12.	**96.** L 9. Takes. White has escaped by means of sacrificing one stone.
97. P 13.	**98.** O 12.
99. N 12.	**100.** O 13.
101. S 12. ("Nozoku.")	**102.** K 12.
103. O 14.	**104.** N 13. ("Shicho.")
105. L 13.	**106.** P 14. Cuts White off.
107. P 15.	**108.** Q 14.
109. Q 15.	**110.** R 14.
111. R 15.	**112.** S 14. All these last moves are obviously necessary.
113. O 15. Connecting.	**114.** S 15.
115. R 16.	**116.** M 14.
	Comment by Honinbo Shuye: "This move is a mistake; it should have been played at M 15."
117. K 14. White's stones in the upper left-hand corner are now connected.	**118.** M 16.
119. G 10. A defensive move. White attempts to get all his stones in one group.	**120.** F 9. ("Tsugu.")
121. J 12. Protects the connection at H 10.	**122.** J 11.
123. J 13.	**124.** N 10. Protecting the "Me" at L 10. K 11 is "Kageme."
125. N 11.	**126.** O 17.
127. L 15.	**128.** M 15. White's situation in the upper right-hand corner looks very bad at this point.
129. Q 17.	**130.** R 18. A better move than Q16.
131. N 17.	**132.** N 18.
133. Q 18.	**134.** S 17.
135. M 17.	**136.** N 16. White is prevented from connecting.

WHITE	BLACK

137. M 18.

138. M 13. Threatening White's other connection.

139. M 12. White must connect.

140. P 18. To an inexpert eye White's group in the upper right-hand corner now looks hopeless.

141. Q 19 This is to prevent "Watari."

142. O 16. Black must play here to protect his four stones.

143. S 16.

144. T 16. ("Watari.")

145. T 15. A sacrifice to prevent Black from forming "Me."

146. T 14. Black must take the stone.

147. R 13. The condition in this corner of the board is now a fine example of "Semeai."

148. S 13.

149. S 18.

150. T 18.

151. S 19. The situation is now highly interesting.

152. R 12. White's sacrifice at T 15 is now bearing fruit.

153. R 17.

154. T 17. Neither side can play at T 19 without loss.

155. P 16. Takes. Forming a perfect "Me," the other being at R 18. The play in this corner is now complete.

156. C 13. Increasing Black's territory.

157. B 5. Protecting the corner.

158. G 13.

159. H 11.

160. L 16.

161. K 16.

162. F 15. Extending Black's frontiers.

163. F 17.

164. J 15.

Comment by Honinbo Shuye : "Black's moves 164 and 166 are both useless. At move 164 Black should have played at D 15."

165. H 16.

166. G 16.

167. H 15.

168. D 15.

169. D 16.

170. D 14.

171. G 15.

172. B 15.

WHITE	BLACK

173. B 16.

174. C 14.   Completing the frontier.

175. P 2.

176. Q 2.

177. Q 1.

178. R 1

179. P 1.

180. R 2.   The usual series of moves in such a situation.

181. C 16.   We might say that the end game commences at about this point.

182. J 2.

183. L 2.

184. K 3.

185. A 7.

186. F 16.

187. G 17.

188. F 13.   The stone at G 13 needs support.

189. H 13.   A very good move to protect White's group.

190. A 8.   Stopping White's invasion.

191. B 6.

192. B 7.

193. A 6.

194. B 8.   The usual moves.

195. B 14.

196. B 13.

197. A 15.   Takes.

198. L 17

199. L 18.   Completing the frontier.

200. M 19.

201. K 18.

202. J 6.   All the rest of the board is practically finished.

203. F 11.

204. E 11.

205. F 16

206. E 15.

207. H 14.

208. G 14.

209. E 5.

210. E 12.

211. H 5.

212. J 5.

213. H 4.

214. J 4.

215. G 3.

216. J 9.

Comment by Honinbo Shuye : "This move is unprofitable. Had Black played at J 8, a very good profit would have been secured."

217. J 8.

218. E 4.

WHITE	BLACK
219. F 5.	220. D 1.
221. C 1.	222. D 6. Black must connect.
223. O 9.	224. M 9.
225. K 13.	226. K 11.
227. J 7.	228. H 6.
229. H 10.	230. G 12.
231. H 12.	232. K 7.
233. N 7.	234. O 8.
235. S 5. By sacrificing one stone White forces Black to fill two spaces.	236. Q 4.
237. T 8.	238. T 7.
239. J 1.	240. K 2.
241. K 1.	242. A 13.
243. L 19.	244. N 19.
245. P 19.	246. O 18.
247. A 14.	248. L 14.
249. K 15.	250. M 5.
251. N 5.	252. K 8.
253. Q 9. ("Ko tsugu.")	

Here the game is left as finished in the published report, but the remaining moves are not all strictly speaking "Dame." There are quite a number of moves to be made before we can proceed to the count. The first question is, naturally, what stones are dead, and we find that White has three dead stones at S 12, S 5, and K 4. Black has three dead stones at J 15, O 4, and R 18. The white stones at P, Q, and R 13, are not dead yet. They have aggressive possibilities, and must be actually surrounded. As near as we can judge the game would proceed as follows:

First : Necessary although obvious moves which are not strictly "Dame."

WHITE	BLACK
	254. O 12. The three white stones must be taken before Black is safe.
255. R 19. White must take this before filling T 19.	**256.** T 15. A necessary connection.
257. N 6. Necessary to form connection.	

Second: The following moves which are strictly "Dame." It makes no difference which side fills these intersections, but it would generally be done as follows:

WHITE	BLACK
	258. T 19.
259. O 19.	**260.** P 17.
261. N 15.	**262.** N 14.
263. F 12.	**264.** J 10.
265. H 7.	**266.** M 7.
267. M 4.	**268.** M 3.

The frontiers are now absolutely in contact, and the count can be made, and it will be seen that after filling up the vacant territory with the captured stones as far as they will go, Black has won by three points. The Japanese would rearrange the board in order to make the counting of the spaces more easy ("Me wo tsukuru"), but for the first game or two the beginner might find it less confusing to omit this process.

Honinbo Shuye comments on this game as follows :

"In spite of so many errors, Black wins showing how great is the advantage resulting from a handicap."

II

Plate 15

WHITE. — Murase Shuho, seventh degree.
BLACK. — Uchigaki Sutekichi, fifth degree.

This game is taken from Korschelt, and the notes are his. In some of these notes will be found mere repetitions of matter that I have inserted in the preceding chapters, or which will be hereafter found in the chapter on " Joseki." These notes are, however, very full and valuable, and a little repetition may have the effect of aiding the memory of the student, and will do no harm. Contrary to the custom, this game was played without handicaps.

BLACK

WHITE

1. R 16. In the beginning of the game the corners and margins are first occupied, because it is there that positions can most easily be taken which cannot be killed, and which also contain territory. From the edges and corners the player makes toward the center. This process is repeated in every game.

2. D 17.

3. Q 3. In taking a corner that is still vacant there is a choice among seven points; *e.g.*, in the corner designated as D 4, these points are D 3, D 4, D 5, C 4, C 5, E 3, and

4. P 17. The attack could also be commenced at P 16.

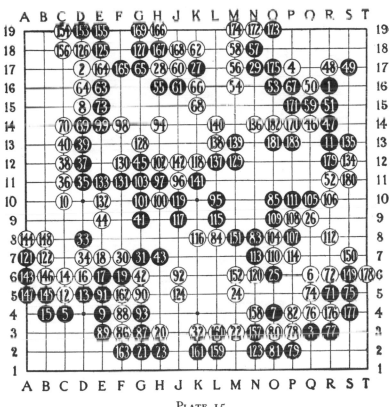

PLATE 15

E 4. On the other hand, C 3 and E 5 are bad, because the territory which is obtained by C 3 is too small, and the adversary would reply to E 5 with D 4, by means of which E 5 would be cut off from the margin. Of moves that are good D 3–C 4 are the surest, and most frequently used. E 4–D 5 formerly were the favorite moves, but the preceding moves are now preferred to them. E 3–C 5 are seldom used. All of this, of course, applies to the corresponding points in the other three corners.

5. C 4.

7. O 4. Beginners would have replied to Q 6 with Q 5 or R 5. They attack their opponent at close quarters from the beginning, because they cannot take in the whole field at a glance. Their entire effort is to absorb the last stone that their opponent has played. When two beginners play together the battle

6. Q 6. Corresponding to No. 4, this move should have been played at R 5 or Q 5, but White plays on Q 6, because if he played on Q 5, Black would have replied at R 10 or R 9, and later White P 5 and Black O 4 would have followed, with the result that White has nothing, while Black has obtained two positions, one on O–Q and the other on R.

8. D 15. The position D 15–D 17 is very strong, and players like to take it. This applies, of course, to the corresponding positions in other parts of the board, of which there are seven; i.e., C 16–E 16, Q 3–Q 5, etc. As soon as one player gets a position of the kind his opponent often takes a similar position on

moves slowly from a corner out over the board, and one side of the board is entirely filled with stones, while the other is completely empty. This is a sure sign of bad play In the beginning the good players spread their stones over the board as much as possible, and avoid close conflicts.

9. E 4.

11. R 13. In place of taking this secure position on line R, Black should have attacked the white stone on P 17 with L 17, and in this way Black would have obtained positions on both line 17 and on line R.

13. D 5.
15. B 4.
17. E 6.
19. F 6.

the next move in order to balance the advantage gained by his adversary; this is something like castling in Chess.

10. C 10. If White did not occupy this point, we might have the following continuation:

B. C 10   W. C 7
B. C 13   W. E 7

and Black has the advantage, because White's stones at C 7–E 7 can only get one "Me" on the edge of the board, and later on must seek a connection with some other group. By constantly harassing such endangered groups territory is often obtained.

12. C 5. White sees that Black plays too carefully, and therefore challenges him with a bold but premature attack that gives the whole game its character.

14. C 6.
16. D 6.
18. E 7.
20. H 3. As soon as Black answers this move, White will take territory on the right or left of H 3.

BLACK

21. G 2. Is played very carefully. K 3 would probably have been better. In that case White would either have played H 5 in order to save H. 3, whereupon

    B. F 7   W. E 8

    B. K 5

would have followed, or White would have answered at K 4.

23. H 2. The only correct answer would have been K 3, which would have separated White's twentieth and twenty-second stones.

25. O 6.

27. K 17. All good players agree that 27 should not have been played at K 17, but at L 17. This is difficult to understand because K 17 can be supported from both

WHITE

22. M 3. Two stones which mutually support each other on the margin of the board and form a position cannot be separated by more than two spaces; for instance, R 13–R 16. In that case the adversary cannot cut one off from the other. (Korschelt here inserts continuations similar to what we have shown in a preceding chapter.) Therefore, White's twentieth and twenty-second moves are merely intended to fill territory that would otherwise fall to Black, and are not intended to form a new group.

24. M 5. White seeks to form a connection with No. 6, which Black frustrates by his twenty-fifth move. It is of the greatest importance to prevent the union of groups which the adversary has formed on the margin, in order that they may remain weak, and require continuous defense.

The player who has the "Sente" most of the time will generally be the victor.

26. Q 9. Is very necessary in order not to surrender the entire right side to Black.

28. H 17. This move has the effect of abandoning stone No. 4 at P 17. After Black's twenty-ninth move at N 17, No. 4 could still escape by means of P 15, but giving

sides at G 17 and N 17, but L 17 is better because Black should be occupied not merely with taking a position, but more particularly with killing White's fourth stone. In the sequel K 17 is actually taken by White.

29. N 17.
31. G 7.

33. D 8.
35. D 11.
37. D 12.
39. D 13.
41. G 9.

it up brings more territory elsewhere than is there lost. It is a favorite device of strong players to apparently abandon a position to their adversary after first preparing it so that eventually it may live, or so that it may afterward aid in surrounding one of the adversary's groups. The abandoned position often reawakens to life if the weaker adversary allows his surrounding group to be itself surrounded and taken before the capture of the abandoned position has been completed.

30. F 7.

32. K 3. It might have been better to have played at G 8. Then if Black replied at H 7, White could play at C 10, and the white territory in the neighborhood of line D would be very large. Certainly in that case H 3 would have been abandoned, but not M 3–M 5. Since 32 K 3 is purely defensive, Black gets the attack, and appreciably reduces the white territory in the neighborhood of line D.

34. D 7.
36. C 11.
38. C 12.
40. C 13.
42. G 6. If this move had not divided the black groups, Black would have become too powerful.

43. H 7.

44. E 9. This connects the two parts of the White position, which connection was threatened by Black's thirty-third stone. Moreover, the "Sente" remains with White, because Black cannot allow his position to be broken into through F 10.

45. G 12.

46. Q 14.

47. R 14.

48. R 17.

49. S 17.

50. Q 16.

51. R 15.

52. R 11. The beginner will wonder that 52 Q 15 did not follow 51 R 15. This is because 53 R 10– 54 R 9 would result, and White would be at a disadvantage. The moves 46–52 are part of a deeply thought-out plan on the part of White. Black could afford to ignore No. 4 as long as it stood alone. Thereupon White increases it by Nos. 48 and 50, and Black must accept the sacrifice, because otherwise Nos. 27–29 are threatened. By this sacrifice White gets the territory around No. 27, and also has an opportunity of increasing his position on line Q by his fifty-second move.

53. O 16.

54. M 16. On the fifty-third move Black proceeds with the capture of Nos. 4, 48, and 50, while White on his fifty-fourth move hems in No. 27.

55. H 16. This move is ignored by White because Black must reply

56. M 17.

to his fifty-sixth and fifty-eighth moves in order to save Nos. 29 and 53.

57. N 18.

59. Q 15.

61. J 16.

63. E 16.

65. G 17.

67. P 16. This is necessary to avoid the following continuation:

 W. P 16, O 15, N 16, O 14

 B. P 15, N 15, O 17, P 18

and White has the advantage.

69. D 14.

71. R 5.

73. E 15. It is of the utmost importance to Black to occupy this point, for otherwise White would press far into his territory through this opening. He goes first, however, on his seventy-first move to R 5, because White must follow, and then to 73, because on this move he loses the "Sente." Black could also have occupied S 5, to which White would have replied with S 6, because otherwise the following continuation would have occurred:

 B. S 5, S 6, S 8, R 8, Q 8

 W. E 15, S 7, T 7, R 7

and the White position is broken up. It is because Black played at E 15 too hastily and without first occupying S 5 that White can break up the Black position by the series of moves Nos. 74–82.

58. M 18.

60. J 17.

62. K 18.

64. D 16.

66. K 16.

68. K 15.

70. C 14.

72. R 6.

74. Q 5. Murase Shuho thought that 74 was a bad move and that S 5 would have been better. The game would then have continued as follows:

 B. 73, E 15, R 4

 W. S 5, S 4

He also thought that White's moves from 76–82 were bad, because nothing in particular was accomplished by separating O 4 from O 6, since it was impossible to kill them.

75. S 5.	**76.** Q 4.
77. R 3.	**78.** P 3.
79. P 2.	**80.** O 3.
81. O 2.	**82.** P 4.
83. N 8.	**84.** L 8.
85. O 10.	**86.** F 3.
87. G 3.	**88.** F 4.
89. E 3.	**90.** G 5.

91. E 5. Black has played on this point because otherwise E 6–F 6 will die; thus,

    W. E 5,   B. F 5 takes
    W. E 5   retakes

92. J 6.

93. G 4. This is intended to secure H 2, G 2 and G 3. The simplest way of doing this would be to play at F 2, but G 4 gains six more "Me" because F 3–F 4 may be regarded as taken.

94. H 14. From this point on, the territory in the center is filled up. Black and White seem to get it in about equal parts.

95. L 10.	**96.** J 11.
97. H 11.	**98.** F 14.
99. E 14.	**100.** H 10.
101. G 10.	**102.** H 12.
103. G 11.	**104.** O 8.
105. Q 10.	**106.** R 10.
107. P 8.	**108.** P 9.
109. O 9.	**110.** O 7.
111. P 10.	**112.** R 8.
113. N 7.	**114.** P 7.
115. L 9.	**116.** K 8.
117. J 9.	**118.** K 12.
119. J 10.	**120.** N 6.

121. A 7. This move is worthy of study.

122. B 7.

123. N 2.

124. J 5.

BLACK	WHITE
125. E 18.	**126.** D 18.
127. G 18.	**128.** G 13.
129. M 12.	**130.** F 12.
131. F 11.	**132.** E 10.
133. E 11.	**134.** S 12.
135. S 13.	**136.** N 14.
137. L 12.	**138.** L 13.
139. M 13.	**140.** L 14.
141. K 11.	**142.** J 12.
143. A 6.	**144.** A 8.
145. B 5.	**146.** B 6
147. A 5.	**148.** B 8.
149. S 6.	**150.** S 7.
151. M 8.	**152.** M 6. Not at M 7, because that would lead to the loss of K 8– L 8.
153. D 19.	**154.** C 19.
155. E 19.	**156.** C 18,
157. N 3.	**158.** N 4.
159. L 2.	**160.** L 3.
161. K 2.	**162.** F 5.
163. F 2,	**164.** E 17.
165. F 17.	**166.** H 19.
167. H 18.	**168.** J 18.
169. G 19.	**170.** P 14.
171. P 15.	**172.** N 19.
173. O 19.	**174.** M 19.
175. O 17.	**176.** R 4.
177. S 4.	**178.** T 6.
179. R 12.	**180.** S 11.
181. O 13.	**182.** O 14.
183. P 13.	

This is as far as the game is recorded in the Go magazine, published by Murase Shuho. A good player can now

foresee the result at the cost of a little trouble.   Black has
won by five points.

According to Korschelt's view, the play would have
proceeded as follows:

	BLACK			WHITE
			184.	T 5.
185.	T 4.		186.	T 7.
187.	S 3.		188.	G 15.
189.	G 16.		190.	J 8.
191.	H 8.		192.	N 13.
193.	N 12.		194.	M 14.
195.	J 7.		196.	K 7.
197.	F 8.		198.	E 8.
199.	D 10.		200.	D 9.
201.	J 15.		202.	J 14.
203.	J 19.	Takes.	204.	K 19.
205.	Q 11.		206.	F 15.
207.	F 16.		208.	J 2.
209.	J 1.		210.	J 3.
211.	M 7.		212.	L 7.
213.	H 4.		214.	J 4.
215.	N 15.		216.	K 9.
217.	K 10.		218.	M 2.
219.	M 1.		220.	Q 13.
221.	M 15.		222.	L 15.
223.	F 9.		224.	Q 12.
225.	P 12.		226.	T 13.
227.	T 14.		228.	T 12.
229.	H 19.			

The stones that are still to be played are "Dame."   By
playing these no "Me" can be either won or lost, and for
the most part it makes no difference whether they are filled
up by Black or White.   These are as follows:

O 15, N 16, H 5, H 6, F 13, E 13, H 5, H 15, F 10, E 13 E 12, H 15, F 10.

Black has sixty-four "Me" and White fifty-seven "Me."

III

BLACK. — Ito Kotaro, fifth degree.

WHITE. — Karigane Junichi, sixth degree.

This game was played in Tōkio about January, 1907, and is a fine illustration of the rule of "Ko." No handicaps were given.

BLACK	WHITE
1. C 4. ("Komoku.") Black being the weaker player, adopts a conservative opening.	**2.** Q 3.
3. D 17.	**4.** C 15.
5. E 3. The opening is conventional so far.	**6.** C 9. This is an unusual move.
7. F 16.	**8.** C 17.
9. C 18.	**10.** D 16.
11. E 17.	**12.** Q 17.
13. R 15.	**14.** R 6.
15. R 11.	**16.** K 3.
17. N 17.	**18.** D 12. Not the best move. P 16 would have been better. This part of the game is generally devoted to the general distribution of stones.
19. P 16. White's stone at Q 17 is now shut in. If the black stone at N 17 were at M 17, White could have escaped.	**20.** P 17
21. O 17.	**22.** S 16.
23. R 16.	**24.** R 17.
25. S 15.	**26.** S 17.

27. P 18.

29. O 19.   Probably not the best.
O 15 would have had greater possibilities.

31. J 16.   Not the best.   O 15
would have been better.

33. Q 15.

35. O 16.

37. R 13.

39. Q 11.

41. P 11.

43. R 8. Not the best move. N 11
would have been more aggressive.

45. K 17.

47. L 16.

49. L 15.

51. K 18.

53. L 18.

55. H 16.

57. H 15.

59. H 14.

61. J 13.

63. O 10.

65. N 10.

67. K 12.   An ineffective move;
B 17 would have been better.

69. B 18.

71. F 18.   Black must defend his
corner, which is already much re-
duced in size.

28. Q 18.

30. S 19.   The corner is a typical
Go problem.   White had to place
this stone very carefully in order to
provide for the necessary two "Me."

32. Q 16.

34. P 15.   Cutting Black's connection.   The necessity for a black
stone at O 15 is now apparent.

36. P 14.

38. Q 12.

40. P 12.

42. M 13.

44. K 16.   White   now   commences a series of moves to break
up Black's territory at the top of
the board.

46. L 17.

48. K 15.

50. J 17.

52. H 17.

54. J 15.

56. G 16.

58. G 15.

60. G 17.

62. O 11.

64. N 11.

66. M 11.

68. B 17.

70. F 15.

72. A 18.

BLACK	WHITE
73. G 19.	**74.** L 14.
75. K 14. The three white stones, J 15, K 15, and K 16 are dead. They were sacrificed in order to break up Black's territory at the top of the board.	**76.** M 15.
77. M 16.	**78.** Q 8.
79. Q 7.	**80.** R 7.
81. P 8.	**82.** S 8.
83. Q 9. Takes.	**84.** R 9.
85. O 13. An effort to deprive the white group of the necessary "Me" and to envelop them.	**86.** O 14.
87. N 13.	**88.** N 14.
89. L 10.	**90.** L 11.
91. K 10. K 11 would not do; White could break through in that case.	**92.** R 12.
93. S 12.	**94.** Q 13.
95. S 10.	**96.** R 14.
97. S 14.	**98.** S 13. Takes.
99. T 13. "Watari."	**100.** L 12.
101. N 12.	**102.** M 10.
103. M 9.	**104.** K 11.
105. J 11. White is now shut in.	**106.** O 12. White saves his group in this way because he can get the position called "Magari shimo-ku wa me" no matter what Black does.
107. R 4.	**108.** Q 4.
109. R 3.	**110.** R 2.
111. S 2.	**112.** Q 2.
113. S 5.	**114.** Q 6.
115. S 1. Black's corner is small, but it will surely live.	**116.** Q 8. Takes. "Ko."

BLACK	WHITE
117. P 7.	**118.** P 9.
119. R 8. "Ko."	**120.** T 3. An effort to destroy the corner.
121. S 3.	**122.** Q 8. "Ko."
123. P 10.	**124.** N 4. White eventually wins the game by means of the territory he now maps out.
125. E 16.	**126.** E 15.
127. D 14. "Nozoku."	**128.** D 15.
129. C 7.	**130.** J 10.
131. L 8.	**132.** H 11.
133. J 12.	**134.** J 9.
135. G 11. Not very good. Black should have played at K 8.	**136.** N 8.
137. N 9.	**138.** K 8.
139. L 9. Black must play here to protect his two stones.	**140.** B 4.
141. B 3.	**142.** D 4.
143. C 3.	**144.** C 5.
145. C 6. An unusual way of playing the corner.	**146.** N 6.
147. L 6.	**148.** K 5.
149. K 6.	**150.** J 5.
151. J 6.	**152.** H 6.
153. H 7.	**154.** G 10.
155. F 11.	**156.** G 7.
157. G 6.	**158.** H 5.
159. G 8.	**160.** F 7.
161. F 8.	**162.** H 8.
163. J 7. Note how the center fills up without either side getting territory there.	**164.** F 10.
165. E 8.	**166.** E 7.
167. E 11.	**168.** E 10.

BLACK	WHITE
169. D 11.	**170.** D 8.
171. D 7.	**172.** F 5.
173. E 5.	**174.** F 6.
175. C 14.	**176.** M 7.

177. R 8. "Ko." A weak move. White's position is already better, and Black should play at B 14, where he might have a chance to kill White's group, in the upper left-hand corner.

178. B 14. White's group is now safe.

179. B 13.	**180.** A 14.
181. C 12.	**182.** B 16. This is an interesting problem. If White plays at B 15, Black could kill the group.

183. L 7.	**184.** D 5.
185. C 8.	**186.** D 9.
187. B 5.	**188.** B 6.
189. A 4. Takes.	**190.** D 6.
191. B 7.	**192.** B 8.
193. A 6. Takes.	**194.** F 2. Defending his large territory on the lower edge of the board.

195. E 4.

196. Q 8. "Ko." Attacking Black's group which has still to form the necessary two "Me."

197. J 8.

198. H 9. White cannot afford to fill the "Ko" at R 8.

199. R 8. "Ko."	**200.** G 18.
201. H 19.	**202.** Q 8. "Ko." Returning to the attack.

203. Q 9. Takes.

204. E 6. A necessary connection.

205. G 4. Invading White's territory.

206. G 5. Takes. White must do this or lose ten stones.

207. E 2.

208. G 3.

BLACK		WHITE	
209. P 6.		**210.** P 5.	
211. M 5.		**212.** N 5.	
213. M 4.		**214.** M 3. This ends Black's invasion.	
215. F 4.		**216.** Q 14.	
217. R 13. "Ko."		**218.** B 19. "Sente."	
219. D 18. Black must connect.		**220.** S 13. "Ko."	
221. R 5.		**222.** Q 5.	
223. R 13. "Ko." Black must win this "Ko" or lose five stones.		**224.** J 18	
225. J 19.		**226.** S 13. "Ko."	
227. L 4. "Sente."		**228.** L 3.	
229. R 13. "Ko." Black's group is now safe.		**230.** H 12.	
231. S 13. "Ko tsugu."		**232.** E 13.	
233. B 10.		**234.** B 9.	
235. F 13.		**236.** E 14.	
237. G 14.		**238.** H 3.	
239. S 6.		**240.** D 3.	
241. D 2.		**242.** C 10.	
243. C 11.		**244.** B 11.	
245. R 8. "Ko."		**246.** M 6.	
247. L 5.		**248.** Q 8. "Ko."	
249. R 1.		**250.** Q 1.	
251. R 8. "Ko."		**252.** S 7.	
253. S 9.		**254.** Q 8. "Ko."	
255. E 12.		**256.** D 13.	
257. R 8. "Ko."		**258.** G 12. "Sen te."	
259. F 12.		**260.** Q 8. "Ko."	
261. F 3.		**262.** G 2.	
263. R 8. "Ko."		**264.** T 4.	
265. T 2. Black must defend his group.		**266.** Q 8. "Ko."	
267. T 16.		**268.** T 17.	
269. R 8. "Ko."		**270.** T 6.	

BLACK	WHITE

271. T 5. Black must stop the White advance. **272.** Q 8. "Ko."

273. Q 19. **274.** R 19.

275. R 8. "Ko." **276.** P 19. "Ko."

277. Q 18. **278.** Q 8. "Ko."

279. S 18. If Black can also play at T 19, White's corner is dead. **280.** T 18.

281. R 8. "Ko." **282.** N 15.

283. L 13. Purposely starting another "Ko." **284.** K 13. "Ko."

285. B 12. **286.** L 13. "Ko tsugu."

287. A 11. Takes. **288.** Q 8. "Ko."

289. C 13. **290.** R 8. "Ko tsugu."

291. K 9. Black must form another "Me" for this group at once. **292.** O 6.

293. J 4. **294.** H 4.

295. K 4. **296.** C 2.

297. B 2. **298.** E 1.

299. C 1. Takes. **300.** J 3.

301. T 9. The game is practically over at this point. **302.** N 16.

303. J 14. Taking three stones. **304.** O 8.

305. T 19. Takes. **306.** O 7.

307. P 9. Connecting. **308.** T 15. Takes.

309. T 8. **310.** C 19.

311. F 17. **312.** A 13.

313. A 12. **314.** A 17.

315. D 19. **316.** A 19.

317. R 10. **318.** A 9.

319. A 10. **320.** Q 19. "Ko tsugu."

321. A 7.

The game as published ends at this point, but there still remain moves to be made that are not strictly "Dame." White must kill the three black stones at E 8, F 8, and G 8, as that portion of the board is not quite disposed of, and "Seki" might easily occur if White plays badly. The game might continue as follows:

BLACK		WHITE	
		322. F 1.	
323. G 13.		**324.** E 9.	
325. H 13.		**326.** H 10.	White must connect.
327. A 8.		**328.** F 9.	
329. D 10.		**330.** G 9.	White must take the three stones.
331. D 1.	Stopping White's advance.	**332.** T 16.	"Tsugu."

The following moves are strictly "Dame":
F 14, H 18, M 8, O 15, T 14. Either side can fill these "Me."

The following stones are dead and can now be removed:

> WHITE. — K 8, L 17, T 3, T 4.
> BLACK. — N 12, N 13, O 13, S 18.

White wins by four stones. After the dead stones are used to fill up the vacant spaces, and the board is rearranged, it will be found that White has fourteen "Me" and Black ten "Me."

More than the usual number of moves were made in this game.

IV

Plate 16

WHITE. — Hirose Heijiro, fifth degree.
BLACK. — Nagano Keijiro, fourth degree.

Black has a handicap of two stones.   (D 4 and Q 16.)
Played March, 1907, in Tokio.   Both players were of the Hoyensha School.

When this game was published, it was annotated by Mr. Iwasaki Kenzo, and I have translated his annotations; these are indicated by the initials "I. K."

WHITE	BLACK
1. R 4.	2. C 16.
3. F 17	4. D 15.
5. C 11. To prevent Black forming territory on the left side.	6. C 7. P 3 would have been better. (Iwasaki Kenzo.)
7. O 3.	8. R 10. This move is called "Moku Shita." It is one of Murase Shuho's inventions.
9. R 14. White breaks into Black's territory at once.	10. R 6.
11. O 17.	12. O 16. These moves will be found in the chapter on "Joseki."
13. N 16.	14. O 15.
15. P 17.	16. Q 17.
17. Q 13. White must look out for the stone at R 14.	18. R 15. This move secures the corner, and at the same time protects the connection of Black's stones on lines O and Q. "Ikkyo ryo toku."
19. O 13.	20. N 14.

WHITE	BLACK

WHITE

21. L 17.   Replies to Black's last move.

23. S 14.

25. G 17.

27. P 10.

29. C 14.

31. C 13.

33. D 11.

35. E 11.

37. F 12.   White cuts off.   This is an aggressive move.

39. G 12.

41. G 13.

43. D 8.   White provides an escape for stones on line 11.

45. H 10.

47. D 7.

49. D 6.

51. F 6.

53. J 10.   White cannot risk jumping farther.

55. H 17.   Not good. K 8 would have been better.   (I. K.)

57. C 8.   Good, but not the best. M 12 would have helped the white stones near the center.

59. J 14.   White retreats.

61. L 14.

63. L 12.

BLACK

22. Q 14.

24. F 16.

26. S 15.   Secures the corner.

28. Q 8.   P 6 would have been better.   (I. K.)

30. D 14.

32. D 12.   Not the best move. M 3 would have been better. (I. K.)

34. E 12.

36. F 11.

38. F 13.   G 14 would have been better.   (I. K.)

40. F 10.

42. F 14.

44. H 15.   H 14 was better, as White dare not cut off at G 14. (I. K.)

46. F 8.

48. C 6.

50. D 5.

52. H 9.   Black must provide an exit for his stones on line E.

54. H 8.

56. K 8.   Black promptly escapes.

58. L 10.   Black commences an attack on White's five stones.

60. J 15.

62. L 15.

64. J 12.   This is a "Sute ishi," but it greatly aids Black's attack.

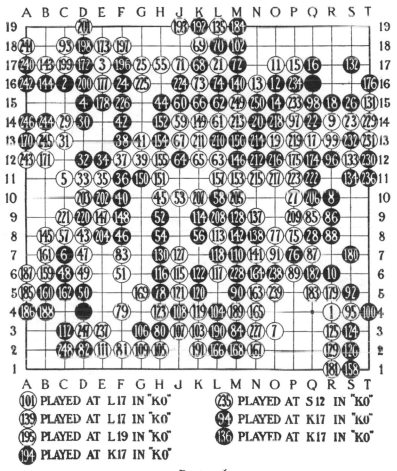

PLATE 16

101 PLAYED AT L17 IN "KO"
139 PLAYED AT L17 IN "KO"
195 PLAYED AT L19 IN "KO"
194 PLAYED AT K17 IN "KO"

235 PLAYED AT S12 IN "KO"
94 PLAYED AT K17 IN "KO"
136 PLAYED AT K17 IN "KO"

65. K 12. Not a good move. By reason of this Black's sixty-eighth move is made possible. (I. K.)

67. J 13. Another move which arrests the development of the game. (I. K.)

69. K 18.

71. J 17.

73. K 16. Takes.

75. P 8. White abandons the field and plays elsewhere.

77. O 8.

79. F 4.

81. F 2.

83. F 7. White perfects his connection.

85. Q 9.

87. Q 7.

89. P 6.

91. O 7. Takes.

93. C 18. Stronger than C 17.

95. S 4.

97. P 14.

99. R 13.

101. L 17. Takes. in "Ko"

103. K 3. Invading Black's territory. White can connect on either side.

105. H 2.

107. J 3.

66. K 15.

68. K 17. Attacks White's stones at the top of the board.

70. L 18.

72. M 17.

74. L 16. Black's attack on the upper right-hand corner is now well developed.

76. P 7.

78. H 5.

80. H 3.

82. D 2.

84. M 3.

86. R 9.

88. R 8.

90. M 5. Black enlarges his territory at the bottom of the board.

92. S 5. Forming "Me" for the side group.

94. K 17. Takes in "Ko."

96. R 12.

98. Q 15.

100. T 4.

102. M 18.

104. L 4.

106. G 3.

108. J 4.

WHITE	BLACK
109. G 2.	**110.** M 7.
111. E 2.	**112.** C 3. If Black plays at D 3, White could reply at D 1 with the "Sente."
113. L 8. Threatening Black's territory. If Black defends, White can connect somewhere.	**114.** K 9.
115. J 6.	**116.** H 6.
117. L 6. White's attack on this territory is very fine.	**118.** L 7.
119. K 4.	**120.** K 5.
121. J 5.	**122.** K 6.
123. H 4. Takes.	**124.** S 3.
125. R 3.	**126.** S 2.
127. J 7.	**128.** M 9. Black cannot neglect this — the whole center of the board might be lost.
129. R 2.	**130.** H 7.
131. T 15.	**132.** S 17. Better than T 16, as it provides for "Me" in the corner.
133. S 12	**134.** S 11.
135. L 19.	**136.** K 17. Takes in "Ko."
137. N 9.	**138.** N 8.
139. L 17. Takes in "Ko."	**140.** M 16.
141. N 7.	**142.** M 8.
143. B 17.	**144.** B 16.
145. B 8.	**146.** M 12. Threatening to surround the ten white stones in the center.
147. E 9.	**148.** F 9.
149. K 14. Forming "Me" for group in center.	**150.** G 11.
151. H 11.	**152.** H 14.
153. M 11.	**154.** H 13.
155. H 12.	**156.** M 13.

WHITE	BLACK
157. L 11.	**158.** S 1. This move is worth five or six points.
159. B 6. B 5 might have been more aggressive.	**160.** B 5.
161. B 7.	**162.** C 5.
163. N 5.	**164.** N 6.
165. N 4.	**166.** L 2.
167. N 2.	**168.** M 2. Otherwise White would play at L 3.
169. G 5.	**170.** A 13. This stone is connected with stone at B 16. This move often occurs.
171. B 12.	**172.** D 17.
173. E 18.	**174.** Q 12.
175. P 12.	**176.** T 16.
177. E 16.	**178.** E 15.
179. R 5.	**180.** S 7.
181. R 1.	**182.** Q 6.
183. Q 5. This part of the board is now completed.	**184.** M 19.
185. A 5.	**186.** A 4.
187. A 6.	**188.** B 4.
189. M 4.	**190.** L 3.
191. K 2.	**192.** K 19. Takes.
193. J 19.	**194.** K 17. Takes in "Ko."
195. L 19. Takes in "Ko."	**196.** F 17.
197. F 18.	**198.** D 18.
199. C 17.	**200.** D 16.
201. D 19. "Watari."	**202.** E 10.
203. D 10.	**204.** E 8.
205. M 10.	**206.** Q 10.
207. K 10.	**208.** L 9. Takes.
209. P 9.	**210.** L 13.
211. K 13.	**212.** N 12.
213. M 14.	**214.** N 13.

WHITE		BLACK	
215. N 11.		**216.** O 12.	
217. O 11.		**218.** O 14.	
219. P 13.		**220.** D 9.	Takes.
221. C 9.		**222.** Q 11.	
223. P 11.		**224.** J 16.	Takes.
225. C 16.		**226.** F 15.	
227. N 3.		**228.** M 6.	
229. T 14.		**230.** T 12.	
231. T 13.		**232.** S 13.	Takes.
233. P 15.		**234.** P 16.	
235. S 12.	Takes in "Ko."	**236.** T 11.	
237. E 3.		**238.** O 6.	
239. O 5.		**240.** A 17.	
241. A 18.		**242.** A 16.	
243. A 12.		**244.** B 14.	
245. B 13.		**246.** A 14.	
247. D 3.		**248.** C 2.	
249. M 15.		**250.** N 15.	

Black wins, the report says, by "Ichi ban," which means anything up to ten "Me." According to my continuation, Black won by seven "Me."

V

Plate 17

This is a game between a Japanese player and a beginner. It is inserted solely to show the character of the mistakes which beginners are likely to make. Such errors never occur in games between good players, and therefore this game may be more useful to a novice than the games contested between players of greater skill.

Played May 7, 1907.

Black has a handicap of five stones.

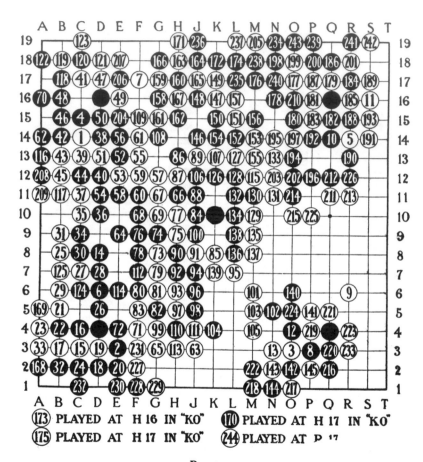

(173) PLAYED AT H 16 IN "KO" (170) PLAYED AT H 17 IN "KO"
(175) PLAYED AT H 17 IN "KO" (244) PLAYED AT P 17

PLATE 17

WHITE	BLACK
1. C 14.	**2.** E 3. Bad; too close to the handicap stone. Besides it is better to respond to White's attack in the same part of the board,
3. O 3.	**4.** C 15. This would be too conservative if the players were anything like equal.
5. R 14.	**6.** D 6. Much better to play in one of the right-hand corners. C 6 would be better also.
7. F 17.	**8.** P 3. O 4 is much better.
9. R 6.	**10.** Q 14.
11. S 16. This would not be played against a good player.	**12.** O 4. Black should reply to White's last move.
13. N 3.	**14.** D 8. Unnecessary; much better to play in one of the threatened corners.
15. C 3.	**16.** C 4. B 4 would be better.
17. B 3.	**18.** D 2.
19. D 3.	**20.** E 2.
21. B 5.	**22.** B 4.
23. A 4.	**24** C 2.
25. B 8.	**26.** D 5. Over cautious.
27. C 7.	**28.** D 7. Unnecessary; Black could gain a decisive advantage at B 6.
29. B 6.	**30.** C 8. Too near the White line, a common mistake of beginners.
31. B 9.	**32.** B 2.
33. A 3.	**34.** C 9. Too near; Black can jump one or two spaces with much better effect.
35. C 10.	**36.** D 10.
37. C 11.	**38.** D 14.
39. C 13.	**40.** D 12. At this point Black's

WHITE	BLACK
	position is good enough, as his line on D is very strong.
41. C 17.	42. B 14.
43. B 13.	44. C 12. Black gains very little by this.
45. B 12.	46. B 15.
47. D 17.	48. B 16. Very bad; Black has the whole board to gain ground in elsewhere.
49. E 16.	50. D 15. If Black feels he must play here, D 13 is better.
51. D 13.	52. E 13.
53. E 12.	54. D 11.
55. F 13.	56. E 14.
57. G 12.	58. E 11.
59. F 12.	60. F 11. If Black hopes to save his group in the upper left-hand corner, he must escape toward the center at this point.
61. F 14. Black's group is now hopeless.	62. A 14. Black cannot possibly form "Me"; this move is merely wasted.
63. J 3.	64. E 9. Too cautious.
65. G 3.	66. H 11.
67. G 11.	68. F 10. Black forms "Me" in this group long before it is threatened, while he might gain ground elsewhere.
69. G 10.	70. A 16. Another lost move.
71. F 4.	72. E 4.
73. G 8.	74. G 9.
75. H 9.	76. F 9.
77. H 10.	78. F 8.
79. G 7.	80. F 6.
81. G 6.	82. G 5. Should have been

WHITE	BLACK

BLACK — played at F 5.

83. F 5.

84. J 10. Black should play nearer the edge of the board. J 10 is radically wrong.

85. K 8.

86. H 13. Black tries to form a living group in the center without support; this can seldom be done.

87. H 12.

88. J 11.

89. J 13.

90. H 8.

91. J 8.

92. H 7. These stones are hopeless from the start. Black should play in the right-hand corners.

93. H 6.

94. J 7.

95. L 7.

96. J 6.

97. H 5.

98. J 5.

99. G 4. Takes.

100. J 9.

101. M 6.

102. N 5. M 5 would be much better.

103. M 5.

104. K 4. Black adds more stones to his already hopeless group. This is one of the commonest mistakes.

105. M 4.

106. J 12. Black should jump to the right, say at M 11.

107. K 13.

108. G 14. F 15 might have helped Black.

109. F 15.

110. H 4.

111. J 4.

112. F 7.

113. H 3. Takes.

114. E 6. Unnecessary. Black should play somewhere in the unoccupied portion of the board.

115. M 12.

116. A 13. Wholly wasted unless Black were an expert.

117. B 11.

118. B 17.

119. B 18.

120. C 18.

WHITE	BLACK
121. D 18.	**122.** A 18.
123. C 19. Takes.	**124.** C 6.
125. B 7.	**126.** K 12. Like all beginners, Black keeps his stones too close together. M 10 would be better.
127. L 13.	**128.** L 12.
129. M 10.	**130.** M 11.
131. N 11.	**132.** L 11.
133. N 13.	**134.** L 10. Black again adds stones to a dead group.
135. M 9.	**136.** L 8.
137. M 8.	**138.** L 9.
139. K 7.	**140.** O 6.
141. P 5.	**142.** O 2. S 4 would have been much better.
143. N 2.	**144.** N 1. Black overlooks that he must connect at P 2. This is a common error of novices.
145. P 2.	**146.** J 14.
147. K 16.	**148.** J 16.
149. K 17.	**150.** K 15. Black tries to form another living group. His only chance was near Q 14–Q 16.
151. L 15.	**152.** L 14.
153. M 14.	**154.** K 14.
155. M 13.	**156.** M 15.
157. L 16.	**158.** G 16. Black again adds to a hopeless position.
159. G 17.	**160.** H 17.
161. G 15.	**162.** H 15. Black thinks he has the necessary "Me." Two of them, however, are "Kageme."
163. H 18.	**164.** J 18.
165. J 17.	**166.** G 18.

WHITE	BLACK

167. H 16. Takes, "Ko."

168. A 2. Black plays this correctly.

169. A 5.

170. H 17. Takes, "Ko."

171. H 19.

172. K 18.

173. H 16. Takes, "Ko."

174. L 18.

175. H 17. "Ko tsugu."

176. M 17. Black has a chance to make some territory in this part of the board.

177. O 17.

178. N 16.

179. Q 17.

180. O 15.

181. P 16.

182. Q 15.

183. P 15.

184. ·R 17.

185. R 16.

186. Q 18.

187. P 17.

188. R 15.

189. S 17.

190. R 13.

191. S 14.

192. P 14.

193. S 15.

194. O 13. Black should live, although he has gained little space.

195. N 14.

196. P 12. Black should have occupied O 14.

197. O 14. Black's groups are now separated.

198. N 18.

199. O 18.

200. P 18.

201. R 18. Takes.

202. O 12.

203. N 12.

204. E 15. This is pure waste.

205. M 19. If Black had played here his group would have lived.

206. E 17.

207. E 18. Takes.

208. A 12.

209. A 11.

210. O 16. Too late; this group is hopeless now.

211. Q 11.

212. Q 12.

213. R 11.

214. O 11.

215. O 10.

216. Q 2.

WHITE	BLACK
217. O 1. Takes.	**218.** M 1. This is nonsense; Black might still save the corner by correct play.
219. P 4.	**220.** Q 3.
221. Q 5.	**222.** M 2. If Black played at S 5 he would still have a chance.
223. R 4.	**224.** O 5.
225. P 10.	**226.** R 12.
227. F 2.	**228.** F 1.
229. G 1.	**230.** E 1.
231. F 3.	**232.** C 1. Black wastes one of his few vacant spaces.
233. R 3.	**234.** N 19.
White permits Black to play again.	**235.** L 17.
White permits Black to play again.	**236.** J 19.
237. L 19.	**238.** M 18.
White permits Black to play again.	**239.** P 19.
White permits Black to play again.	**240.** N 17.
White permits Black to play again.	**241.** R 19.
242. S 19.	**243.** O 19.
244. R 17.	

"Dame" — E 5 and C 5.   White wins by one hundred and ninety-seven spaces and eighty-eight stones.

VI

Plate 18

WHITE. — Inouyé Inseki.
BLACK. — Yasui Shintetsu.

Played December, 1835. No handicaps were given. This game is from a Japanese work called "Kachi Sei Kioku." The notes are taken from Korschelt, and as in the previous instance involve the repetition of some things that have been touched on in the preceding chapters.

BLACK	WHITE
1. R 16.	**2.** D 17.
3. Q 3.	**4.** P 17.
5. C 4.	**6.** C 14. Just as good as D 15, which we already know.
7. Q 5. This may be the best play under the circumstances. The secure position Q 3–Q 5 supports the advance posts at C 4 and R 16 in equal measure.	**8.** Q 14,
9. P 16.	**10.** Q 16.
11. Q 15.	**12.** Q 17.
13. P 15.	**14.** R 15.
15. R 14.	**16.** S 15.
17. Q 13.	**18.** N 17. The eighth stone played at Q 14 cannot be saved. If White attempts to save it, the following would be the continuation:

BLACK   WHITE

B.	W.
	P 14
O 14	P 13
P 12	O 13
N 13	O 12.
O 11 etc.	

If White had had an opportunity of placing a stone on the line of retreat at say E 3, then White could have saved No. 8. (This has already been explained in defining the Japanese expression "Shicho.")

19. P 14. Takes. S 14 probably would have been better, because it would have retained the "Sente" for Black; that is to say, a play which the opponent is compelled to answer, or otherwise sustain too great a loss. Had Black played at S 14, White must have answered at S 16, in order not to lose the stones at R 15–S 15, and also the corner, which is worth about fourteen "Me." To White's play at S 16 Black would probably have answered at R 12 and thus obtained a secure position.

20. S 16.

21. R 9.

23. J 3.

22. E 3.

24. D 5. This is analogous to No. 8, but it is not advanced so far because Black has already occupied J 3.

25. C 5.

27. C 6.

29. C 7.

26. D 6.

28. D 7.

30. D 8.

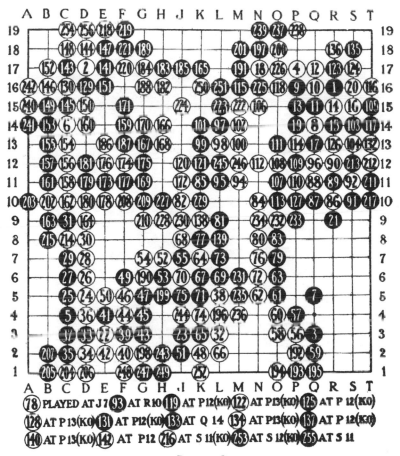

78 PLAYED AT J 7 · 93 AT R 10 · 119 AT P 12(KO) · 122 AT P 13(KO) · 125 AT P 12(KO)
128 AT P 13(KO) · 131 AT P 12(KO) · 133 AT Q 14 · 134 AT P 13(KO) · 137 AT P 12(KO)
140 AT P 13(KO) · 142 AT P 12 · 216 AT S 11(KO) · 253 AT S 12(KO) · 255 AT S 11

PLATE 18

31. C 9.

32. L 3. White has established the long line on D and allowed Black a large territory in order to be able to occupy L 3. If he had played there immediately in answer to Black's twenty-third move, then either L 3 or E 3 would have been in great danger.

33. D 3.	**34.** D 2.
35. C 2.	**36.** D 4.
37. C 3.	**38.** L 5.
39. F 3.	**40.** F 2.

41. E 4. Black compels White to take 41, in order to make good his escape.

42. E 2.

43. G 3.	**44.** F 4.
45. G 4.	**46.** F 5.
47. G 5.	**48.** K 2.
49. F 6. "Sente."	**50.** E 5. Takes.
51. J 2.	**52.** H 7.
53. H 6.	**54.** G 7.
55. J 7.	**56.** P 3.
57. P 4.	**58.** O 3.
59. Q 2.	**60.** O 4.
61. O 5.	**62.** N 5.
63. O 6.	

64. K 7. An interesting attack that determines the course of the game for a long time. 65 J 8, would mean abandoning the position on G–J (26 "Me"), but it would give an opportunity for a bold attack. If Black played 65, J 6, his stones would scarcely survive.

65. K 3. "Sente." White must

66. L 2.

reply to it, or he would find himself without the necessary "Me" in
that group.

67. K 6.

69. L 6.

71. K 5. Avoids "Ko" and
nevertheless assures a connection.

73. L 7.

75 J 5.

77. K 8.

79. O 7.

81. L 9.

83. O 8.

85. K 11.

87. Q 10.

89. R 11.

91. S 10. Takes.

93. R 10. Q 12 would probably
have been better; at all events it
would have been surer, because it
assures the connection by way of
P 11 after White has taken. If
White does not take, but plays at
P 11, his stones on the edge of the
board will die.

95. L 11.

97. L 14.

99. K 13.

101. K 14.

103. S 14.

105. T 15.

107. O 11. It is certain that

68. J 8.

70. J 6. Takes.

72. N 6.

74. K 4. Is played for the same
reason as No. 66.

76. N 7.

78. J 7.

80. N 8.

82. J 10.

84. N 10.

86. R 10. Now the effect of the
mistake at move 19 begins to be
apparent.

88. Q 11.

90. R 12.

92. S 11.

94. M 11. This move separates
P 14 from K 11, and is at the same
time "Sente" as regards the black
stones near K, because if Black
does not answer, these stones would
be cut off by W–K 10. Moves Nos.
98, 100, and 102 isolate the black
stones in the neighborhood of P 14.

96. Q 12.

98. L 13.

100. M 13.

102. M 14.

104. S 13.

106. N 15.

108. O 12.

either the eight black stones or the
five white stones must die, and on
this depends the result of the game,
because it would make a difference
of about 40 "Me."

BLACK	WHITE
109. P 12.	**110.** P 11.
111. O 13.	**112.** N 12.
113. O 10.	**114.** P 13. Takes, "Ko."
115. M 16.	**116.** T 16.
117. T 14.	**118.** O 16.
119. P 12. "Ko."	**120.** J 12.
121. K 12.	**122.** P 13. "Ko."
123. R 17.	**124.** S 17.
125. P 12. "Ko."	**126.** R 13.
127. P 10.	**128.** P 13. "Ko."
129. D 16.	**130.** C 16.
131. P 12. "Ko."	**132.** T 13.
133. Q 14. Connecting.	**134.** P 13. "Ko."
135. S 18.	**136.** R 18. Takes.
137. P 12. "Ko."	**138.** K 9.
139. L 8.	**140.** P 13. "Ko."
141. E 17.	**142.** P 12. Connecting. White would have had another "Ko" at M 10.
143. C 17.	**144.** D 18.
145. C 15.	**146.** B 16.
147. E 18.	**148.** C 18.
149. B 15.	**150.** D 15.
151. E 16.	**152.** B 17. Takes. The series of moves from 143 to 152 should be carefully noted, as they frequently occur.
153. B 14.	**154.** C 13.
155. B 13.	**156.** C 12.
157. B 12.	**158.** C 11.

BLACK	WHITE
159. F 14. "Sente."	**160.** D 14.
161. B 11.	**162.** C 10.
163. B 9. Is not played at B 10 in order to retain the "Sente" without conceding too great an advantage.	**164.** D 9. It would have been better to play at K 17.
165. K 17.	**166.** H 14.
167. G 13.	**168.** H 13.
169. G 11.	**170.** G 14.
171. F 15.	**172.** J 11.
173. E 11.	**174.** F 12.
175. G 12.	**176.** E 12.
177. F 11.	**178.** E 10.
179. D 11.	**180.** D 10.
181. D 12.	**182.** H 16.
183. H 17.	**184.** G 17.
185. J 17.	**186.** E 13.
187. F 13.	**188.** G 16.
189. G 18.	**190.** G 6.
191. M 17.	**192.** P 2.
193. P 1.	**194.** O 1.
195. Q 1	**196.** L 4.
197. N 18.	**198.** G 2. "Sente." It threatens the three black stones on J and K.
199. H 5.	**200.** O 18.
201. M 18.	**202.** B 10.
203. A 10.	**204.** C 1.
205. B 1.	**206.** D 1.
207. B 2.	**208.** F 10. C 8 ought to have been occupied first.
209. G 10.	**210.** G 9.
211. T 11.	**212.** T 12.
213. S 12. Takes.	**214.** C 8.
215. B 8.	**216.** S 11. "Ko."

BLACK		WHITE	
217. T 10.		**218.** E 19.	
219. F 19.		**220.** F 17.	
221. F 18.		**222.** M 15.	
223. L 15.		**224.** J 15.	
225. N 16.		**226.** O 17.	
227. H 10.		**228.** H 9.	
229. K 10.		**230.** J 9.	
231. M 6.		**232.** O 9.	
233. P 9.		**234.** N 9.	
235. M 5.		**236.** M 4.	
237. O 19.		**238.** P 19.	
239. N 19.		**240.** A 15.	
241. A 14.		**242.** A 16.	
243. H 2.		**244.** J 4.	
245. L 12.		**246.** M 12.	
247. G 1.		**248.** F 1.	
249. H 1.		**250.** K 16.	
251. L 16.		**252.** K 1.	
253. S 12.	"Ko."	**254.** C 19.	
255. S 11.	Connecting.	**256.** D 19.	

White wins by seven stones.

VI

"JOSEKI" AND OPENINGS

From the earliest times the Japanese have studied the opening of the game. Especially since the foundation of the Go Academy there have been systematic treatises on this subject, and for keen and thorough analysis, these treatises have nothing to fear from a comparison with the analogous works on Chess openings. There is, however, a difference between the opening of the game in Chess and the opening in Go, because in the latter case the play can commence in each of the four corners successively, and therefore, instead of having one opening, it might be said that there are four.

The Japanese masters usually overcome this difficulty by treating a corner separately, as if it were uninfluenced by the position or the possibility of playing in the adjacent corners, and in their treatises they have indicated where the first stones in such an isolated corner can advantageously be played. These stones are called " Joseki." As a matter of fact, these separate analyses or " Joseki" differ slightly from the opening of the game as actually played, because it is customary in opening the game to skip from one corner to another, and the moment a few stones are played in any corner the situation in the adjacent corners is thereby influenced. It is due to this fact also that in their treatises on the " Joseki" the Japanese writers do not continue the analysis as far as we are accustomed to in our works on Chess. While this method of studying the openings persists to the present time, one of the greatest of the Japanese masters, Murase Shuho, compiled a series of openings which correspond more closely to our Chess openings; that is to say, the game is commenced, as in actual play, all over the board, and is not confined to the study of one corner as in the case of the conventional " Joseki." Korschelt, in his work on the game, inserts about fifty of these openings by Murase Shuho, with notes that were prepared by the Japanese master especially for the use of foreigners, and I have selected a few of these in addition to the collection of " Joseki" which we will first consider.

The work from which my " Joseki" have been selected was compiled by Inouye Hoshin, and published in November, 1905. It was originally written for the "Nippon Shimbun," a newspaper published in Tokio. Of course, the annotations accompanying these " Joseki" are not the original ones from the Japanese text. Many of the things which I point out would be regarded as trite and obvious to a good player, and my annotations are intended solely to aid beginners in understanding some of the reasons for the moves given. It must also be understood that the series of " Joseki" which I have inserted falls far short of completeness. In a Japanese work on the game there would be at least five times as many.

Although the " Joseki" have been studied by the Japanese masters from the earliest times, it does not mean that the ordinary player in Japan is familiar with them; just as in this country we find a majority of Chess players have a very limited acquaintance with the Chess openings, so in

Japan many players attain a fair degree of skill without a thorough acquaintance with the "Joseki." It would certainly very greatly aid the beginner in attaining proficiency if he were to study these examples, and follow them as nearly as possible in actual play.

It would seem to us that in compiling a work on "Joseki," or openings, we would commence with the openings where no handicap is given, and later study those where there were handicaps; it is another instance of the divergent way in which the Japanese do things that they do just the opposite, and commence their treatises with the study of openings where handicaps are given. Inasmuch as this is a book on a Japanese subject, I shall follow their example and shall commence the study of "Joseki" in games where Black has a handicap.

As we have already seen, the handicap stone is always placed on a certain fixed point, which is the fourth intersection from the edge of the board in each direction, and White has five recognized methods of playing his first stone in relation to such handicap stone. These are called "Kogeima kakari," "Ogeima kakari," "Daidaigeima kakari," "Ikken taka kakari," "Nikken taka kakari." We shall take up examples of these in their order.

I

HANDICAP

Plate 19 (*A*)

WHITE	BLACK
1. R 14. "Kogeima kakari." This is the most usual move for attacking the corner. The purpose of	2. N 17. This move supports the handicap stone and also gains as much ground as possible for Black.

WHITE

White's first move is to lay a basis for future aggression; he cannot, of course, play in the corner immediately, neither can he play nearer the black stone with advantage.

3. R 17. This is a direct attack on the corner. White can either connect with his first stone or form a living group in the corner.

5. S 16. White threatens to connect.

7. S 17. White cannot play at R 15 at this time because he would lose the stone at S 16.

9. P 18. Since White cannot connect, he must play to form two "Me" in the corner.

11. Q 17. White makes his corner as large as possible. This move is also "Sente," because it threatens to break through Black's line.

13. S 14. White threatens "Watari," and again Black must reply at once. ("Sente.")

15. Q 14. To confine Black's group and prepare for territory on the right side of the board.

BLACK

Beginners would generally find O 17 more safe and conservative.

4. R 16. Black plays to prevent the connection of the white stones.

6. S 15. Black breaks the connection by this move.

8. R 15. Black also must connect. Beginners are prone to neglect these necessary connecting moves.

10. P 17. Black plays to connect his stones, and at the same time confines White to the corner.

12. O 17. Black must connect to prevent White's escape.

14. T 14. Prevents "Watari."

16. P 15. An important defensive move. Otherwise White could almost envelop the black stones.

Even game. White has a small territory in the corner, but Black has greater possibility of expansion.

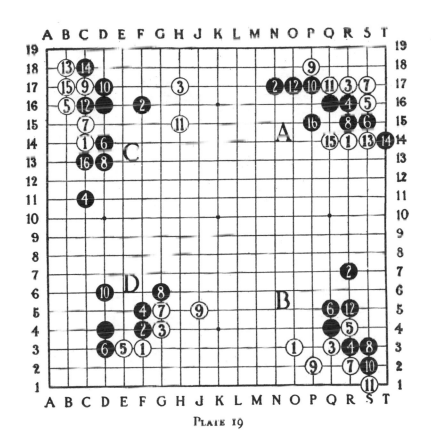

PLATE 19

II

HANDICAP

WHITE	BLACK
1. R 14.	**2.** N 17.
3. R 17.	**4.** R 16.
5. Q 17. In place of trying to connect as before, White threatens to extend in the other direction.	**6.** P 16. Black prevents White from getting out.
7. S 16. Threatens to connect again.	**8.** S 15. Black stops it again.
9. ·S 17.	**10.** R 15.
11. O 18. White again must form "Me" in the corner.	**12.** O 17.
13. N 18. White extends as far as possible.	**14.** M 18. Black stops the advance.
15. P 17. White must look out for the safety of the stones at N and O 18.	**16.** M 17. Black must connect.
17. P 14. To prevent Black's extension and form a basis for territory on right side.	**18.** O 14. Black extends as far as he can.
19. O 13.	**20.**· N 14.

Again White has the corner and Black has better opportunities for expansion.

III

HANDICAP

Plate 19 (*B*)

WHITE	BLACK
1. O 3.	**2.** R 7.
3. Q 3. This variation is called	**4.** R 3.

WHITE

"Kiri Kaeshi." This move does not attack the corner so aggressively as the preceding examples.

5. R 4. This is the characteristic move of this variation.

7. R 2. White threatens the black stone. If Black defends White can divide the corner.

9. P 2. "Kake tsugu." If White does not make this move, Black will get the "Sente" with a superior position.

11. S 1. White cannot neglect this move. If Black were allowed to play at R 1, he would get the better game.

BLACK

6. Q 5. This is an important move for Black; if he plays elsewhere, he will get a bad position.

8. S 3.

10. S 2. Formerly S 4 was given as Black's move, but it is not so good, because White replies at R 8 with a fine attack.

12. R 5.

In this opening the corner is about evenly divided.

IV

HANDICAP

WHITE

1. R 14.

3. P 14. Preparing for "Kiri Kaeshi" on the other side of handicap stone.

5. P 16.

7. Q 17. "Kiri Kaeshi." The effect of this move is generally to divide the territory.

9. Q 18.

BLACK

2. N 17.

4. R 11. Called "Tenuki." Not necessarily played at R 11. The word means that Black "draws out" and plays in another part of the board.

6. P 17.

8. R 17.

10. R 18.

White	**Black**
11. P 18.	**12.** O 17.
13. R 16.	**14.** Q 15.
15. S 18.	**16.** R 15.
17. S 16.	**18.** S 15.
19. S 17.	**20.** P 15.

White has the corner, but Black has better chances to make territory later.

V

Handicap

Black is supposed to have another handicap stone at D 4.

Plate 19 (*C*)

White	**Black**
1. C 14. "Kogeima."	**2.** F 16. "Ikken taka hiraki." This "Joseki" was an invention of Murase Shuho.
3. H 17. White confines Black's advances.	**4.** C 11. Black prepares to get territory on left side of the board.
5. B 16. White plays to take the corner.	**6.** D 14.
7. C 15.	**8.** D 13. Better than D 15, as it confines White more effectively.
9. C 17.	**10.** D 17.
11. H 15.	**12.** C 16.
13. B 18.	**14.** C 18.
15. B 17.	**16.** C 13. A very good move; it shuts White in the corner and assures Black a large territory on the left side of the board.

This opening might be continued as follows:

WHITE	BLACK
17. D 18.	**18.** E 18.
19. C 19. Takes.	**20.** D 7.

or

WHITE	BLACK
17. C 6.	**18.** D 18.
19. B 13.	**20** B 12.
21. B 14	**22.** C 8.

VI

HANDICAP

Black is supposed to have stones at O 4 and Q 4 also; these are called "Shiki ishi."

WHITE	BLACK
1. F 3. "Kogeima."	**2.** H 3. By this move Black at once attacks the white stone and also prepares to connect with the stone at O 4.
3. F 5. White must get out towards the middle of the board.	**4.** L 3. "Tenuki"; that is, it has nothing to do with the corner in dispute; Black feels he has an opportunity to take territory. It is interesting to note that if the "Shiki ishi" at O 4 were at N 3, then Black would play No. 4 at H 5.
5. D 6. White attacks the handicap stone.	**6.** D 2. This is an important defensive move.
7. E 2.	**8.** B 5. Black tries to escape.
9. B 6.	**10.** C 6.
11. C 5. C 7 would be good also.	**12.** C 7.

White	Black
13. B 4.	**14.** D 5.
15. C 4.	**16.** C 3.
17. B 7.	**18.** C 8.
19. E 6. White must support stone at D 6.	**20.** A 5. This is a very well considered move for Black.
21. A 4.	**22.** B 3.
23. A 6. Takes two.	**24.** B 8.
25. A 3. The corner is now an example of "Semeai"; the question is which side can kill the other first.	**26.** B 2.
27. A 2.	**28.** B 1.
29. D 1.	**30.** A 8. If Black plays at C 1, the corner will become "Seki," as it is, the white group is dead.

Black has much the best of this variation.

VII

Handicap

Black is supposed to have a handicap stone at Q 4 also.

Plate 19 (*D*)

White	Black
1. F 3.	**2.** F 4. "Tsuke te." Again Black takes the aggressive from the start.
3. G 4.	**4.** F 5.
5. E 3.	**6.** D 3.
7. G 5.	**8.** G 6.
9. J 5. White's best move.	**10.** D 6.

Black has the better position.

VIII

HANDICAP

Plate 20 (*A*)

WHITE	BLACK
1. O 17. "Kogeima."	**2.** O 16. "Tsuke te."
3. N 16.	**4.** O 15.
5. Q 17.	**6.** P 17.
7. P 18.	**8.** P 16.
9. N 18.	**10.** R 17.
11. Q 18.	**12.** N 15.
13. M 16.	**14.** R 10. Black abandons stone at R 17 in order to get territory; an amateur might be tempted to play No. 14 at R 18, but in that case White could spoil Black's chance to get space on the right side of the board.
15. R 16.	**16.** R 15.
17. S 16.	**18.** S 15.
19. S 17.	**20.** P 10.

White has the corner, but Black has practically secured a large territory on the right.

IX

HANDICAP

WHITE	BLACK
1. R 14.	**2.** Q 14. "Tsuke te."
3. Q 13.	**4.** P 14.

WHITE	BLACK
5. O 17. White attacks from the other side also.	**6.** R 15,
7. R 13.	**8.** P 18.
9. N 16.	**10.** S 14.

Black has the corner.   White has a chance on both sides.

X

HANDICAP

WHITE	BLACK
1. R 14. "Kogeima."	**2.** Q 14. "Tsuke te."
3. Q 13.	**4.** P 14.
5. O 17. White attacks from the other side as before.	**6.** O 16. Black responds from the outside as in the case of move No. 2.
7. P 17.	**8.** Q 17.
9. P 16.	**10.** R 13.
11. R 15.	**12.** Q 15.
13. R 12.	**14.** S 13.
15. S 12.	**16.** N 17.
17. N 16.	**18.** O 15.
19. M 17.	**20.** N 18.
21. M 18.	**22.** N 13.
23. M 16.	**24.** T 13.
25. Q 12.	**26.** S 15.

Black has the corner and also an outlet to the center. White has a chance to form territory on both sides.   Black's position is preferable.

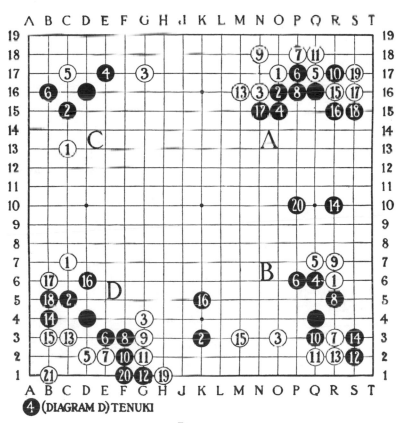

④ (DIAGRAM D) TENUKI

PLATE 20

XI

Handicap

Black is supposed to have a stone at D 4 also.

Plate 20 (*B*)

White	Black
1. R 6.	**2.** K 3. This move is an invention of Murase Shuho; it would not be played unless Black had a stone at D 4. Black's intention is to develop territory in either corner depending on the nature of White's attack.
3. O 3. White attacks the right-hand corner from both sides.	**4.** Q 6.
5. Q 7.	**6.** P 6.
7. R 3. This is a direct attack on the corner.	**8.** R 5. Black must play here before playing at Q 3. It also gives Black the "Sente."
9. R 7. White must connect.	**10.** Q 3.
11. Q 2.	**12.** S 2. This is a clever move. Amateurs would be tempted to play at P 2, which would be very bad for Black, as White would then get the entire right side.
13. R 2.	**14.** S 3. Secures Black's connection with R 5.
15. M 3. White must extend his boundaries or his stones will die.	**16.** K 5. Black plays to shut in White as much as possible; he also supports his stone at D 4.

Black has the better game.

XII

HANDICAP

Plate 20 (*C*)

WHITE	BLACK
1. C 13. "Ogeima Kakari." This is another method of commencing the attack; it does not attack the corner so directly, but it gives White a better chance on the sides or center.	**2.** C 15. This is to prevent White from playing at B 16.
3. G 17. White attacks from the other side in the same way.	**4.** E 17. Preventing White from entering at D 18; this secures the corner for Black.
5. C 17. This is a "Sute ishi" or sacrificed stone. White threatens to connect it with one side or the other.	**6.** B 16.

The game is about even; if White does not play at C 17 on the fifth move, Black gets much the better of it.

XIII

HANDICAP

WHITE	BLACK
1. N 17. "Ogeima Kakari."	**2.** P 17. Preventing the entry at Q 18.
3. R 14. White attacks the other side with "Kogeima."	**4.** S 15. Very important move for Black; if Black makes a move elsewhere at this point ("Tenuki,") White gets much the better of it.

XIV

HANDICAP

Plate 20 (*D*)

WHITE	BLACK
1. C 7.	2. C 5.
3. G 4. "Nikken taka kakari." This is another method of attacking from the other side.	4. E 2. A very important move; if Black plays "Tenuki," White can at once enter the corner.

Suppose Black does not play No. 4, E 2, but plays elsewhere, then the following continuation might occur:

WHITE	BLACK
	4. "Tenuki."
5. D 2.	6. E 3.
7. E 2.	8. F 3.
9. G 3.	10. F 2.
11. G 2.	12. G 1.
13. C 3.	14. B 4.
15. B 3.	16. D 6. Black must get out toward the center.
17. B 6. Threatening "Watari."	18. B 5.
19. H 1.	20. F 1.
21. B 1. By means of this move the white stones in the corner live.	

White has the better of it.

XV

HANDICAP

WHITE	BLACK
1. N 17.	2. P 17.
3. Q 14. This is another method	4. O 15. Black plays to get out

WHITE

of attack, called "Ikken taka ka-kari"; it does not give White a base for attacking the corner immediately.

5. N 15. White also plays out toward the center, otherwise Black would shut him in at M 16.

7. M 15.

9. Q 13.

11. R 11. Beginners might play at Q 12; this is always bad play.

13. L 15.

Even game.

BLACK

toward the center, as White's third move does not menace the corner.

6. N 14.

8. P 13. Amateurs might play at O 14; the text move protects the connection and extends also.

10. P 12.

12. M 14.

14. S 15. Protecting the corner against the white stone at Q 13.

XVI

HANDICAP

Plate 21 (*A*)

WHITE

1. M 17. "Daidaigeima"; not so much used as the other attacks.

3. R 14. "Kogeima." White attacks from the other side.

5. P 16. White threatens the connection between the handicap stone and No. 2, otherwise Black would play at R 12, with the advantage.

7. P 17.

9. O 16.

11. O 18.

BLACK

2. O 17. Black defends the corner from that side.

4. S 16. Black again prevents the advance into the corner.

6. P 15. P 17 looks like the obvious defense, but this would shut Black in the corner and give White the better game.

8. Q 17.

10. P 18.

12. O 15.

WHITE	BLACK

13. N 16. Much better than immediately taking the single black stone.

14. Q 13. This attacks the white stone at R 14; it also defends the connection at Q 15.

15. R 12. Much better than R 13; in that case White would lose both stones.

16. R 13.

17. S 13.

18. Q 14.

Black has the better of it.

XVII

HANDICAP

WHITE	BLACK

1. H 3.

2. F 3.

3. C 6.

4. C 5. This is an alternative method of defending the corner.

5. D 6.

6. F 5. Black plays to avoid being shut in the corner, also it can be demonstrated if he neglects this move his stones will be killed.

7. F 6.

8. H 4.

9. J 4.

10. H 5.

11. G 3.

12. F 2. This is a good move. F 4 would be weak. The text move defends and at the same time threatens White's stones on line 3. F 4 would give White a chance to play elsewhere ("Tenuki") which is a great advantage.

13. J 3.

14. E 5. Black cannot neglect this move, or White can break in with a winning attack.

Again Black has the better of it. He has a chance to

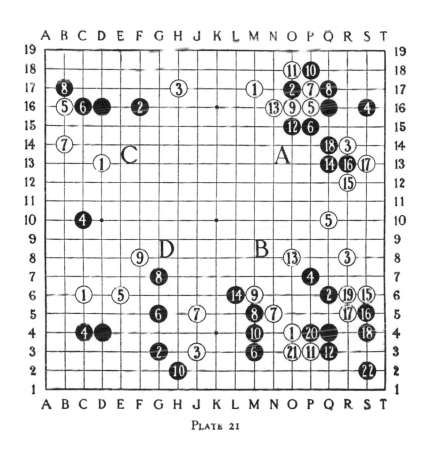

PLATE 21

play at J 1 on the next move. The relation of this stone to the stone at F 2 when at the edge of the board is called "Ozaru," or the "great monkey," and it generally gains about eight spaces. This is also shown among the examples of end positions.

XVIII

HANDICAP

WHITE	BLACK
1. C 8.	**2.** C 6.
3. E 2. This is another method of trying to get in the corner.	**4.** D 2.
5. D 3.	**6.** E 3. This is the crucial move of this variation; if Black plays No. 6 at C 3, he gets the corner, but White gets the better game.
7. C 3.	**8.** C 2.
9. C 4.	**10.** D 5.
11. F 2.	**12.** B 3.
13. B 4.	**14.** B 2.
15. G 4.	**16.** E 4.

Black has the better of it.

XIX

HANDICAP

Plate 21 (*B*)

WHITE	BLACK
1. O 4. "Ikken taka kakari." This is the fourth method of commencing the attack.	**2.** Q 6. This is Black's best answer.

WHITE	BLACK
3. R 8.	**4.** P 7. Black intends to follow up this move on one side or the other, the two points being Q 9 and M 3 This is called "Hibiku," or " to echo "
5 Q 10. White defends on one side.	**6.** M 3.
7. N 5. White must get out.	**8.** M 5.
9. M 6.	**10.** M 4.
11. P 3.	**12.** Q 3.
13. O 8.	**14,** I 6
15, S 6	**16.** S 5.
17. R 5.	**18.** S 4.
19. R 6.	**20.** P 4.
21. O 3.	**22.** S 2. Black prepares to form "Me" in the corner.

White must now play at Q 6 to save his stones on the left side.

This " Joseki" is very much spread out; it is difficult to say who has the better of it.

XX

HANDICAP

WHITE	BLACK
1. D 14.	**2.** C 14. Not so good as F 16.
3. C 15. This is not White's best move; it is done to confuse Black, and will win if Black does not know how to reply.	**4.** D 15.
5. C 13.	**6.** B 14.
7. B 15.	**8.** B 13. D 13 would be bad.

WHITE	BLACK
9. C 17.	**10.** D 17.
11. C 18.	**12.** C 12.
13. D 13.	**14.** D 18.
15. D 19.	**16.** C 16.
17. B 16.	**18.** A 15.
19. A 17. A 16 would not do.	**20.** E 19.
21 C 19.	**22.** F 18. "Kake tsugu." Black must protect his connection; this situation arises frequently.
23. B 18. White plays on the only point to save the corner.	**24.** F 15.
25. D 12.	**26.** C 11.
27. D 11.	**28.** C 10.

Black has the better game.

XXI

HANDICAP

Plate 21 *(C)*

WHITE	BLACK
1. D 13. "Nikken taka kakari"; this is the fifth method of opening the attack.	**2.** F 16. Black has a variety of moves at his command; the text move is probably best.
3. H 17.	**4.** C 10. Really "Tenuki." Black can play equally well at C 7.
5. B 16.	**6.** C 16.
7. B 14.	**8.** B 17.

Black has the corner and White has commenced to envelop his stones. The following continuation might occur:

WHITE	BLACK
5. F 18.	**6.** D 18.
7. E 17.	**8.** C 15.

Black's last move in this continuation is interesting, because it will make "Kake tsugu" no matter which way White tries to break through. If he should play at D 17, White could get through at E 16.

XXII

HANDICAP

WHITE	BLACK
1. N 16.	2. O 17. This is an alternative defense.
3. N 17.	4. O 16.
5. O 15.	6. N 18. This is Black's best move. If he plays at P 15, White replies at O 18 with a good attack.
7. M 18.	8. O 18.
9. M 15.	10. N 14. This stone will be sacrificed, but while White is killing it Black gets advantage elsewhere.
11. N 15. White must connect.	12. Q 14.

Black has the better of it.

XXIII

HANDICAP

WHITE	BLACK
1. G 4.	2. D 7. This is another defensive move.
3. D 3.	4. E 3. This is better than C 3; in that case Black gets the worst of it.
5. E 4.	6. C 3.
7. D 2.	8. E 5.
9. F 4.	10. C 4. C 2 is not so good.
11. C 2.	12. B 2.

<table>
<tr><td>WHITE</td><td>BLACK</td></tr>
<tr><td>**13**. E 2. White must look out for his three stones. B 1 would be a bad move.</td><td>**14**. C 10.</td></tr>
</table>

The corner is divided, but Black has better prospects.

XXIV

HANDICAP

WHITE	BLACK
1. F 3.	**2**. C 7.
3. C 9.	**4**. D 3. Black's three stones are now called "Ogeima shimari"; they are supposed to be a strong formation protecting the corner.
5. C 5. The point of this variation is to show that White can strike in on this move and yet live.	**6**. D 5.
7. C 6.	**8**. D 7.
9. B 7.	**10**. B 8.
11. B 6.	**12**. C 8.
13. D 6.	**14**. E 6.
15. E 7. White threatens from the outside.	**16**. C 4.
17. B 9.	**18**. E 8. Black cannot venture A 8, as his four stones would then die.
19. A 8. "Watari."	**20**. F 7. Takes.

White has entered the corner and still his stones will live.

XXV

HANDICAP

Plate 21 (*D*)

WHITE	BLACK
1. C 6.	**2.** G 3.
3. J 3.	**4.** C 4.
5. E 6. Instead of entering the corner, White attacks from both sides.	**6.** G 5. Black tries to get out toward the center; this move also prevents White from playing at E 3.
7. J 5.	**8.** G 7.
9. F 8.	**10.** H 2.

Black has a good game.

We now come to the "Joseki" where no handicaps are given. In such cases, of course, Black has the first move. The first stone is generally played on an intersection adjacent to the point on which the handicap stone is placed when given. There are, therefore, eight intersections on which the first stone might be played. In the lower left-hand corner, for instance, these would be C 3, C 4, C 5, D 3, D 5, E 3, E 4, F 5. By common consent C 3 has been rejected as disadvantageous for the first player, because the territory obtained thereby is too small. E 5 has been rejected because it allows the adversary to play behind it and take the corner. D 4, or the handicap point, is also not used. The other six points may be divided into duplicate sets of three each, and, therefore, there are only three well-recognized methods of playing the first stone. These are: in the lower left-hand corner, C 4 or D 3, the most usual and conservative, which is called "Komoku," or the "little 'Me'"; E 4 or D 5 which is bolder, called "Takamoku," or the "high 'Me'"; and E 3 or C 5 which is not so much used as either of the others, called "Moku hadzushi," or the "detached 'Me.'" We shall give about an equal number of examples of each of these methods of opening the game, commencing, as is customary in the Japanese works, with "Takamoku."

I

No Handicap

Plate 22 (*D*)

BLACK	WHITE
1. D 5. "Takamoku." This is the most aggressive of the three methods of opening.	**2.** D 3. This is White's best answer. E 3 is also good. C 3 is bad.
3. C 3. Black plays to get territory on the left; he attacks from inside.	**4.** C 2. Best; if he attempts to cut off at C 4 he gets a bad game.
5. C 4. Black extends.	**6.** E 2. Necessary to secure the connection at D 2.
7. C 9. Black takes territory on left side.	**8.** G 4. White takes space to the right.

Even game.

II

No Handicap

BLACK	WHITE
1. Q 15 "Takamoku."	**2.** Q 17.
3. P 17. Black attacks from the outside.	**4.** P 18.
5. P 16.	**6.** O 17. White plays to get territory on one side or the other; he

BLACK

WHITE

will sacrifice one of his stones on line 17.

7. O 18. This stone is intended as a sacrifice to aid Black in getting the corner. It is better than Q 18.

8. N 18. White plays to secure the left-hand side.

9. Q 18. Black now secures the corner.

10. O 19. Takes.

11. R 17.

12. O 16. An important stone; it is played to secure White territory on the left, also to aid in an attack on the right-hand side.

13. P 14. This is also important as it extends Black's territory; he cannot neglect it.

14. K 16. White returns to his original plan and secures territory to the left.

Even game.

Suppose Black neglects P 14 on his thirteenth move, we would then have the following continuation:

BLACK

WHITE

	BLACK		WHITE
13.	"Tenuki."	**14**.	P 14.
15.	Q 14.	**16**.	Q 13.
17.	R 13.	**18**.	R 12.
19.	Q 12.	**20**.	P 13.
21.	R 11.	**22**.	S 12.
23.	S 11.	**24**.	S 13.
25.	R 14.	**26**.	Q 11.
27.	P 12.	**28**.	S 10.
29.	R 10.	**30**.	Q 10.
31.	R 9.		

White has the better of it.

III

No Handicap

Plate 22 (*A*)

BLACK	WHITE

1. P 16. "Takamoku."

2. R 16.

3. Q 14. The purpose of this move is to confine White to the corner.

4. P 17. White tries to get out on the left.

5. O 17. Black prevents this.

6. Q 17.

7. O 16.

8. R 14. White tries the other side.

9. R 13. Black stops him.

10. S 14.

11. Q 16. If Black wishes "Tenuki," this is good, otherwise S 13 would be better.

12. R 17.

13. E 17. "Tenuki," but, nevertheless, played with reference to the stones on line O.

Even game. White has the corner, but Black has better possibilities.

IV

No Handicap

BLACK	WHITE

1. E 16. "Takamoku."

2. C 16.

3. D 14.

4. E 17.

5. D 16. Black threatens to break into the corner.

6. D 17.

7. C 17 Black repeats his threat; in reality it is a sacrificed stone.

8. B 17.

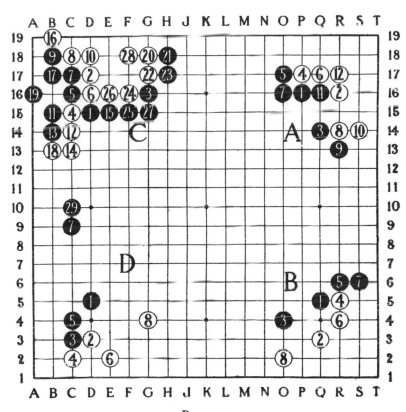

PLATE 22

BLACK	WHITE
9. C 18. This stone may be lost, but it aids Black in attacking from the outside.	**10.** B 18. White must play here to save his stones.
11. C 15.	**12.** B 16.
13. F 17.	**14.** D 18.
15. E 18.	**16.** C 19. Takes two.
17. G 16.	

This is an old "Joseki" which used to be popular; it fell into disuse and was revived by Murase Shuho. It is good enough for White if he has an outlying stone or two in the neighborhood, otherwise it is bad play for White.

V

No Handicap

The following stones are supposed to be on the board: Black, Q 13, R 13, R 15; White, Q 14, P 16, Q 17.

BLACK	WHITE
1. Q 5. Black plays "Taka-moku," thinking to connect with stones on line 13.	**2.** R 3. White plans to prevent Black's connection and reduce the Black territory.
3. P 3. This is an error; if Black wishes to frustrate White's plan, R 4 is the correct play.	**4.** Q 4.
5. P 4.	**6.** R 5.
7. R 6.	**8.** S 6.
9. R 7.	**10.** S 7.
11. R 8.	**12.** S 8. White has now made a formidable attack on the Black territory.
13. R 9.	**14.** P 5. If Black gets this point, his line would be too strong.
15. Q 6.	**16.** Q 2. Important; not merely

BLACK

WHITE

to attack Black on line P, but it prevents Black from coming to R 2, which would mean 10 "Me"; it also prepares for O 2.

White has the better of it.

Variation commencing at White's sixteenth move:

BLACK	WHITE
	16. O 5. Not so good as No. 16, Q a.
17. R 2.	18. S 2.
19. Q 2.	20. S 4. White secures the necessary two "Me."
21. M 3.	

Black now has secured territory at the bottom of the board and confined White to the corner with the better game.

VI

NO HANDICAP

Plate 22 (*B*)

BLACK	WHITE
1. Q 5.	2. Q 3.
3. O 4.	4. R 5.
5. R 6.	6. R 4.
7. S 6.	8. O 2.
9. "Tenuki" at Q 15.	

White has the corner; Black can afford "Tenuki" at move nine because if White cuts at Q 6 Black can still get a good game. In fact Q 15 indirectly defends the connection at Q 6.

VII

No Handicap
Plate 22 (*C*)

BLACK	WHITE
1. D 15.	**2.** D 17.
3. G 16. Old "Joseki," originated by Konno Genko in the Middle Ages.	**4.** C 15.
5. C 16.	**6.** D 16.
7. C 17.	**8.** C 18.
9. B 18.	**10.** D 18.
11. B 15.	**12.** C 14.
13. B 14.	**14.** C 13.
15. E 15.	**16.** B 19.
17. B 17.	**18.** B 13.
19. A 16. This gives Black two "Me."	**20.** G 18.
21. H 18.	**22.** G 17.
23. H 17.	**24.** F 16.
25. F 15.	**26.** E 16.
27. G 15.	**28.** F 18. Important move for defense.
29. C 10.	

Black has the better of it.

VIII

No Handicap

Plate 23 (*A*)

BLACK	WHITE
1. P 17. "Moku hadzushi"; not so much used as the other two open-	**2.** Q 15. This is called "Taka-moku kakari"; it is one of the two

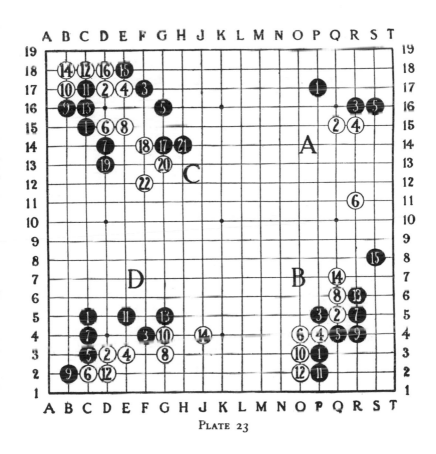

PLATE 23

BLACK	WHITE
ings. It is more conservative than "Takamoku."	general methods of replying to "Moku hadzushi."
3. R 16. Black plays to secure the corner.	**4.** R 15.
5. S 16. The corner is now safe.	**6.** R 11. S 15 would be good also.

Even game.

IX

No Handicap

BLACK	WHITE
1. R 15. "Moku hadzushi."	**2.** P 16.
3. P 15. Black plays to confine White.	**4.** O 15.
5. P 14. Necessary to prevent White breaking in.	**6.** Q 16. White plays to get the corner.
7. R 16.	**8.** N 16. Very important; if neglected, Black gets the corner, and also destroys White's adjacent territory.
9. R 10.	**10.** R 17.
11. S 17.	**12.** S 18.
13. R 18.	**14.** Q 17.
15. S 16.	**16.** K 17.

The corner is evenly divided, and neither side has an advantage.

X

No Handicap

BLACK	WHITE
1. P 17.	**2.** Q 15. "Takamoku kakari."
3. P 15.	**4.** P 16. This is an invention of Murase Shuho.
5. O 16. Black cannot play at Q 16 without getting a very bad position.	**6.** Q 16.
7. Q 17.	**8.** R 17.
9. R 18.	**10.** S 16.
11. S 18.	**12.** O 17.
13. N 17.	**14.** O 18.
15. P 18.	**16.** N 18. This and the two preceding stones are sacrificed; Black naturally expects White to cut at O 15. The text move is a brilliant invention of Murase Shuho.
17. M 17. Black cannot neglect this move.	**18.** O 15.
19. N 16.	**20.** P 14. Takes.
21. K 17. Defensive; Black loses the " Sente."	**22.** R 10.

White has much the better game.

XI

No Handicap

Plate 23 *(B)*

BLACK	WHITE
1. P 3. " Moku hadzushi."	**2.** Q 5. "Takamoku kakari."
3. P 5.	**4.** P 4.

BLACK	WHITE
5. Q 4. This is not a good move for Black and will result in his getting a confined position.	**6.** O 4.
7. R 5.	**8.** Q 6.
9. R 4.	**10.** O 3.
11. P 2.	**12.** O 2.
13. R 6.	**14.** Q 7.
15. S 8. Black cannot play at R 8, as White would cut at R 7.	**16.** E 3.

White has the better position.

XII

No Handicap

Plate 23 (*C*)

BLACK	WHITE
1. C 15.	**2.** D 17. "Komoku kakari." This is the alternative method of defense to this opening.
3. F 17. Black attacks from both sides.	**4.** E 17. This is the crucial move. White plays thus first to get a strong position on line 17, also to prepare for getting out at D 15. Two connected stones always form a strong base.
5. G 16.	**6.** D 15.
7. D 14.	**8.** E 15.
9. B 16. Black now invades the corner; he wishes to occupy C 17, an important point.	**10.** B 17.
11. C 17.	**12.** C 18.
13. C 16.	**14.** B 18.

BLACK	WHITE
15. E 18.	**16.** D 18.
17. G 14.	**18.** F 14.
19. D 13. Guarding the connec-	**20.** G 13.
tion at C 14	
21. H 14.	**22.** F 17

Black has the better position. This is an old "Joseki." It is not much liked at the present time.

XIII

No Handicap

BLACK	WHITE
1. C 15.	**2.** D 17.
3. F 16. This is a variation; the intention is to confine White to the margin.	**4.** E 17.
5. E 15. This is to prevent White from coming to D 15.	**6.** G 17.
7. H 16.	**8.** H 18. This is a correct move. H 17 would inferior.
9. G 16.	**10.** K 17.

Even game.

XIV

No Handicap

Plate 23 (D)

BLACK	WHITE
1. C 5.	**2.** D 3.
3. F 4.	**4.** E 3.
5. C 3. This is unusual; E 5 is the customary move.	**6.** C 2.

Black	White
7. C 4.	**8.** G 3.
9. B 2.	**10.** G 4.
11. E 5.	**12.** D 2.
13. G 5.	**14.** J 4.

Even game; the corner is divided.

XV

No Handicap

Plate 24 (*A*)

Black	White

1. R 16. This move, called "Komoku" is the most frequently used opening when there are no handicaps; it is also the safest for the weaker player.

2. P 17. White's best reply.

3. N 17. This move is called "Ikken basami"; this is the most usual way of continuing: it gives Black an attack at once.

4. R 17. White plays to get the corner.

5. S 17.

6. Q 16.

7. R 15. Black must extend; R 18 would be bad.

8. R 18. White must do the same; he cannot play at S 18.

9. Q 13.

10. S 18. White cannot neglect this move after Black plays at Q 13; if Black had played at R 12, White could have played elsewhere.

Black has the better position.

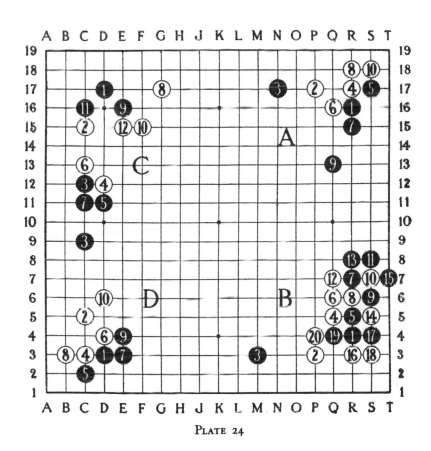

PLATE 24

XVI

No Handicap

BLACK	WHITE
1. Q 17. "Komoku."	**2.** R 15.
3. R 13. "Ikken basami."	**4.** Q 13. This time White does not try for the corner, but attacks the black stone at R 13.
5. Q 12.	**6.** Q 14.
7. N 17. Black abandons the stone at R 13 in order to get greater territory; if he defends it at R 11, White plays at N 17 with a better game.	**8.** R 12.
9. R 11.	**10.** S 12.
11. Q 11. S 11 would be bad.	**12.** S 13.
13. R 16.	**14.** S 15.

Black has the better position.

XVII

No Handicap

BLACK	WHITE
1. D 3. "Komoku."	**2.** C 5.
3. C 7.	**4.** H 3. White in turn attacks the black stone at D 3; G 3 would be too near.
5. D 5. Black connects his stones and shuts White in.	**6.** D 4.
7. E 4.	**8.** C 4.
9. D 6.	**10.** C 3.
11. E 2.	**12.** D 2.
13. E 3.	**14.** L 3. White can afford to

BLACK

WHITE

play for a greater space, as his
stones in the corner will live even
if he loses the stone at D 2.

15. B 6.

16. B 5.

17. C 2.

18. B 2.

19. D 1. Takes.

20. B 1.

Even game.

XVIII

No Handicap

Plate 24 (B)

BLACK

WHITE

1. R 4. "Komoku."

2. P 3.

3. M 3. "Nikken basami." This
is the second variation in this
opening.

4. Q 5. White plays to get out
toward the center.

5. R 5.

6. Q 6.

7. R 7.

8. R 6.

9. S 6.

10. S 7. "Sute ishi."

11. S 8.

12. Q 7.

13. R 8. It would be bad play
to take immediately.

14. S 5.

15. T 7. Takes.

16. R 3.

17. S 4.

18. S 3. This move is made to
secure "Me" in the corner.

19. Q 4.

20. P 4.

The game is about even.

XIX

No Handicap

BLACK	WHITE
1. C 4. "Komoku."	**2.** E 3.
3. H 3. "Nikken basami."	**4.** D 5. White attacks the stone at C 4.
5. D 4.	**6.** E 4.
7. E 5. This is a bad move if White replies correctly, otherwise Black gets the better of it.	**8.** D 6.
9. F 5.	**10.** D 2. This is an important move; it attacks the black stones on line 4 and also prepares for White to extend at G 4. C 2 would be bad, as Black would play at F 4.
11. B 6. Black defends his threatened position.	**12.** G 4.
13. F 7.	**14.** D 8. White must extend.
15. B 2.	**16.** H 4.

Black's third stone at H 3 is now called "Uke ishi," or a "floating stone." White has the better position.

XX

No Handicap

Plate 24 *(C)*

BLACK	WHITE
1. D 17. "Komoku."	**2.** C 15.
3. C 12. "Nikken basami."	**4.** D 12. White attacks the stone at C 12 in this variation.
5. D 11.	**6.** C 13.

BLACK	WHITE
7. C 11.	**8.** G 17. White attacks the other black stone.
9. E 16.	**10.** F 15.
11. C 16. The old book move was E 15, but this gave "Tenuki" to White.	**12.** E 15.

Even game.

XXI

No Handicap

BLACK	WHITE
1. C 4. "Komoku."	**2.** E 3.
3. J 3. "Sangen basami." This move attacks the white stone but not so directly as the preceding variation. It is the invention of Honinbo Dosaku.	**4.** R 4. White takes advantage of his opportunity and plays in another corner.
5. D 3.	**6.** E 4.
7. B 6.	**8.** J 5.
9. M 3. It will be seen in this variation that the stones are played farther apart than in the preceding "Joseki."	**10.** H 3.
11. H 2.	**12.** H 4.
13. D 8. This is an important move for Black.	**14.** O 3.
15. M 5.	**16.** L 4. "Nozoku." It threatens Black's connection on lines M and 3.
17. L 3. If Black defends at M 4, White replies at K 2.	**18.** G 2.

BLACK	WHITE
19. J 2.	**20.** L 5.
21. M 4.	**22.** P 5.

This "Joseki" really deals with two corners.

XXII

No Handicap

Plate 24 (*D*)

BLACK	WHITE
1. D 3. "Komoku."	**2.** C 5.
3. C 9. "Sangen basami."	**4.** C 3.
5. C 2.	**6.** D 4.
7. E 3.	**8.** B 3.
9. E 4. Preparatory to 11 at C 15; generally No. 9 is played at H 3.	**10.** D 6. A good move. E 5 would be bad, because Black would reply at D 6 with a better game.
11. C 15. (Not in diagram.)	

We will now insert ten examples of *openings*, as distinguished from "Joseki." As already stated, these are by Murase Shuho. In these examples Black is supposed to make the best possible moves, and therefore White always finds himself at a disadvantage.

I

Plate 25

Black has a handicap of four stones.

WHITE	BLACK
1. R 14.	**2.** Q 14.
3. Q 13.	**4.** P 14.

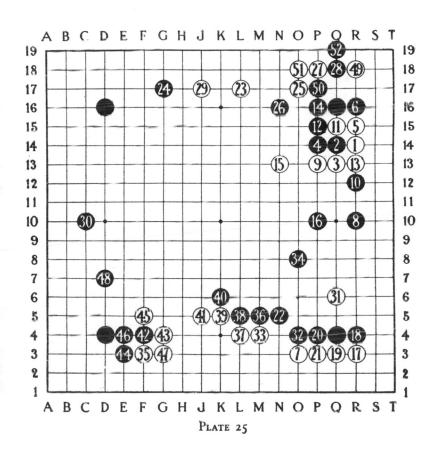

PLATE 25

5. R 15.

7. O 3.

6. R 16.

8. R 10. Formerly in such a case as this Black played at R 7. This move replied to White's move at O 3 and at the same time from a distance attacked White's stones at R 14 and R 15. It is better to confine the last two stones by the text move.

9. P 13.

11. Q 15.

13. R 13.

15. N 13.

17. R 3.

10. R 12.

12. P 15.

14. P 16.

16. P 10. This move is better than R 7.

18. R 4. This move is better than Q 3, which although it cuts off O 3 and R 3 would leave Black's stone at R 10 weak.

19. Q 3.

21. P 3.

23. L 17.

25. O 17.

27. P 18.

20. P 4.

22. N 5.

24. G 17.

26. N 16.

28. Q 18. Black is quite satisfied to have merely the necessary two "Me" in this corner, because he has a much larger territory to the left.

29. J 17.

31. Q 6.

33. M 4. This move is better than O 7 because Black could follow at N 3 in that case. Q 6 is a "Sute ishi" or sacrificed stone. It has the effect of forcing Black to play 34 O 8, and later on will help

30. C 10.

32. O 4.

34. O 8.

WHITE	BLACK

still further to narrow down Black's territory. At the same time every attack on the Black position from the outside would be made more effective by the presence of this stone, Possibly it could also be used later in "Ko." Black makes his 36th, 38th and 40th moves in order to secure his position which is weakened by the presence of the white stone at Q 6.

WHITE	BLACK
35. F 3.	36. M 5.
37. L 4.	38. L 5.
39. K 5.	40. K 6.
41. J 5.	42. F 4.
43. G 4.	44. E 3.
45. F 5.	46. E 4.
47. G 3.	48. D 7.
49. R 18. Beginners would play	50. P 17.
at S 16 or Q 17.	
51. O 18.	52. Q 19.

II

Plate 26

Black has a handicap of four stones.

WHITE	BLACK
1. R 14.	2. Q 14.
3. Q 13.	4. P 14.
5. R 15.	6. R 16.
7. R 10.	8. K 17.
9. O 3.	10. G 3.
11. H 17.	12. F 17.
13. M 17.	14. O 17.

WHITE	BLACK
15. O 18.	**16.** P 17.
17. K 18.	**18.** L 18.
19. L 17.	**20.** J 18.
21. K 16.	**22.** J 17.
23. J 16.	**24.** H 18.
25. M 18.	**26.** P 3.
27. O 4.	**28.** Q 6. This move has the same effect as R 6.
29. J 3.	**30.** C 10.
31. C 6.	**32.** C 4.
33. C 8.	**34.** E 10.
35. F 7.	**36.** G 5.
37. C 12.	**38.** D 7.
39. D 8.	**40.** C 11. This move is very important because it prevents the stone at C 12 from making a connection with that at C 8.
41. E 12.	**42.** F 9.
43. F 8.	**44.** H 9.
45. H 7.	**46.** H 12.
47. C 14.	**48.** K 19.
49. M 15.	**50.** J 5.
51. K 7.	**52.** K 9.
53. L 3.	**54.** R 8.

III

Plate 27

Black has a handicap of three stones.

WHITE	BLACK
1. R 4.	**2.** P 3.
3. L 3.	**4.** G 3.
5. Q 3.	**6** P 4.

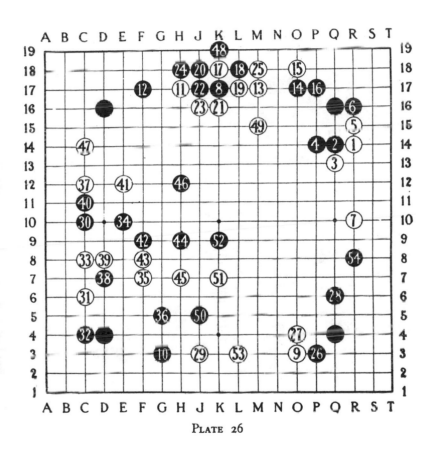

PLATE 26

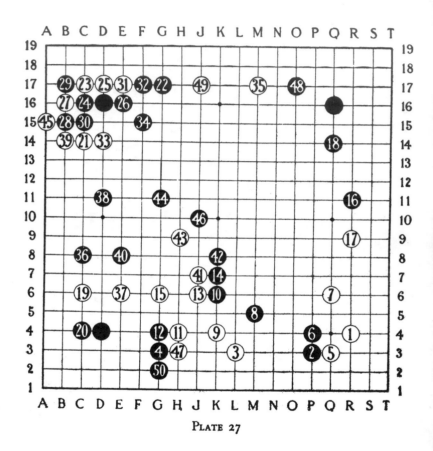

PLATE 27

WHITE	BLACK
7. Q 6.	**8.** M 5. The following is also good.

B. I. 5, M 3, M 4
W. J 3, M 2, Q 8

White playing at Q 8 in order to prevent Black from playing at R 5.

WHITE	BLACK
9. K 4.	**10.** K 6.
11. H 4.	**12.** G 4.
13. J 6.	**14.** K 7.
15. G 6.	**16.** R 11. Black cannot play at R 5 without seeing P 3 and 4 cut off.
17. R 9.	**18.** Q 14.
19. C 6.	**20.** C 4.
21. C 14.	**22.** G 17.
23. C 17.	**24.** C 16.
25. D 17.	**26.** E 16.
27. B 16.	**28.** B 15.
29. B 17.	**30.** C 15.
31. E 17.	**32.** F 17.
33. D 14.	**34.** F 15.
35. M 17.	**36.** C 8.
37. E 6.	**38.** D 11.
39. B 14. The ordinary answer to this is A 14, but this time Black cannot play in this way since White would follow at B 12 and thus threaten the black stones at C 8 and D 11.	**40.** E 8.
41. J 7.	**42.** K 8.
43. H 9.	**44.** G 11.
45. A 15. Black could not occupy A 14 on his 42d and 44th moves.	**46.** J 10.
47. H 3.	**48.** O 17.
49. J 17.	**50.** G 2. This move is necessary.

for the security of the Black position, and at the same time Black does not lose the "Sente" by this move.

IV

Plate 28

Black has a handicap of three stones.

WHITE	BLACK
1. R 14.	**2.** R 5.
3. P 4.	**4.** Q 3.
5. P 3.	**6.** Q 2.
7. R 7. Formerly in this case White played at L 3 and Black replied at Q 6.	**8.** R 6.
9. Q 7.	**10.** P 5.
11. O 17.	**12.** Q 14.
13. Q 13.	**14.** P 14.
15. R 15.	**16.** R 16.
17. P 13.	**18.** O 16.
19. N 16.	**20.** P 17.
21. O 18.	**22.** O 13.
23. O 12.	**24.** O 14.
25. K 17.	**26.** L 3.
27. C 14. At this move White abandons P 3 and 4. If he replied to Black L 3, then there would follow:	**28.** L 5.

B. L 3, L 4, L 5, L 6, G 4
W. M 4, M 5, M 6, M 7
and Black has a decisive advantage.

| **29.** C 8. | **30.** C 6. |

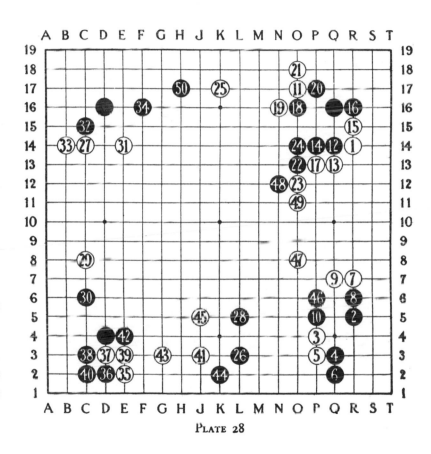

PLATE 28

WHITE	BLACK
31. E 14.	**32.** C 15.
33. B 14.	**34.** F 16.
35. E 2.	**36.** D 2.
37. D 3.	**38.** C 3.
39. E 3.	**40.** C 2.
41. J 3.	**42.** E 4.
43. G 3.	**44.** K 2. The importance of this move, when a territory merely **has** the protection of L 3–L 5, has been commented on before.
45. J 5.	**46.** P 6.
47. O 8.	**48.** N 12.
49. O 11.	**50.** H 17.

V

Plate 29

Black has a handicap of two stones.

WHITE	BLACK
1. R 4.	**2.** D 15.
3. D 17.	**4.** F 16.
5. C 15.	**6.** C 14.
7. C 16.	**8.** D 14.
9. C 8. F 17 is just as good.	**10.** E 18.

Then would follow:

        B. G 17
        W. F 18

WHITE	BLACK
11. D 18.	**12.** P 3.
13. L 3.	**14.** P 6.
15. R 7.	**16.** J 3.
17. L 5.	**18.** J 5.
19. L 7.	**20.** R 3.
21. S 3.	**22.** Q 4. This move and 24– R 2 are necessary because of the white stones on line L.

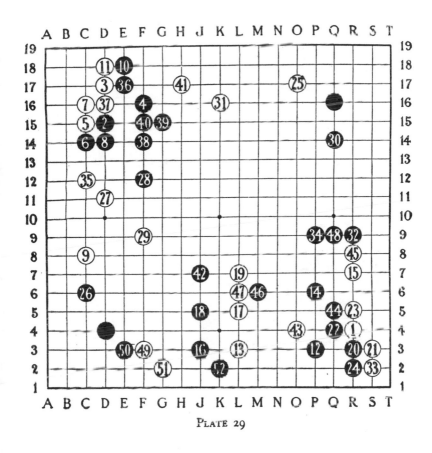

PLATE 29

WHITE	BLACK
23. R 5.	**24.** R 2.
25. O 17.	**26.** C 6.
27. D 11.	**28.** F 12. This move is very good, otherwise White plays at E 16 and breaks into the Black position.
29. F 9.	**30.** Q 14.
31. K 16.	**32.** R 9.
33. S 2. If Black plays at R 9, this move is necessary for the security of the white group.	**34.** P 9.
35. C 12.	**36.** E 17.
37. D 16.	**38.** F 14.
39. G 15.	**40.** F 15.
41. H 17.	**42.** J 7.
43. O 4.	**44.** Q 5.
45. R 8.	**46.** M 6.
47. L 6.	**48.** Q 9.
49. F 3.	**50.** E 3.
51. G 2. This is a fine move. By means of it Black is compelled to play at K 2 and White can occupy F 5 on his 53d move and thus escape, whereas without G 2 White could only have played at F 4, whereupon Black could have cut off the retreat at F 6.	**52.** K 2.

VI

Plate 30

Black has a handicap of two stones.

WHITE	BLACK
1. Q 3.	**2.** D 17.
3. C 15.	**4.** C 13.
5. J 17.	**6.** D 15.

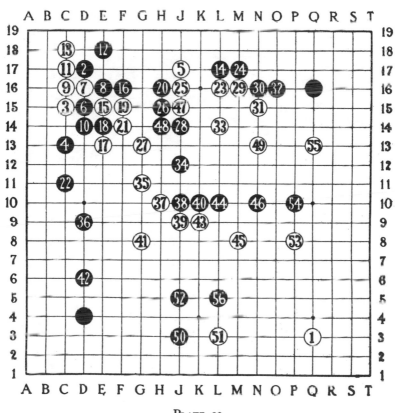

PLATE 30

WHITE	BLACK
7. D 16.	**8.** E 16.
9. C 16.	**10.** D 14.
11. C 17.	**12.** E 18.
13. C 18.	**14.** L 17. Black could prevent White's next move of E 15 by playing 14–G 15.
15. E 15.	**16.** F 16.
17. E 13.	**18.** E 14.
19. F 15. "Shicho" is impossible because White already occupies Q 3.	**20.** H 16. This move makes the Black position secure.
21. F 14.	**22.** C 11.
23. L 16.	**24.** M 17.
25. J 16.	**26.** H 15.
27. G 13.	**28.** J 14.
29. M 16.	**30.** N 16.
31. N 15.	**32.** O 16.
33. L 14.	**34.** J 12.
35. G 11.	**36.** D 9.
37. H 10.	**38.** J 10.
39. J 9.	**40.** K 10.
41. G 8.	**42.** D 6.
43. K 9.	**44.** L 10.
45. M 8.	**46.** N 10.
47. J 15.	**48.** H 14.
49. N 13.	**50.** J 3. White could not occupy this point without endangering the upper position.
51. L 3.	**52.** J 5.
53. P 8.	**54.** P 10.
55. Q 13.	**56.** L 5. Black does not need to further defend his position E 17–P 10, because it surely has two "Me."

VII

No Handicap

Plate 31

BLACK	WHITE
1. C 4.	2. Q 3.
3. D 17.	4. E 3.
5. D 5.	6. R 16.
7. R 5.	8. O 17.
9. F 4.	10. G 3.
11. O 4.	12. O 3. From here the game might continue as follows:

B.	W.
N 3	P 4
O 2	P 3
N 4	Q 6
R 7	K 3

but this is bad for Black.

BLACK	WHITE
13. P 4.	14. P 3.
15. N 4. M 3 would be just as good.	16. R 4.
17. N 3.	18. S 5.
19. J 3.	20. C 11. White abandons the stones at E 3 and G 3. If he were to play at G 4, Black would reply at C 11 with too great an advantage.
21. C 14.	22. C 8.
23. D 3.	24. J 17.
25. G 17.	26. J 15.
27. J 5. Now the two white stones are cut off.	28. Q 12.
29. L 15. Black cannot venture any farther in.	30. L 17.
31. P 16.	32. P 17.
33. Q 16.	34. Q 17.

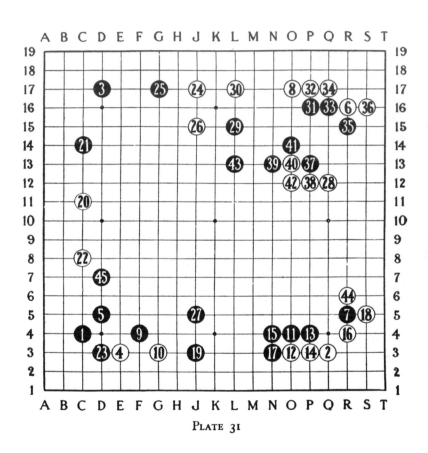

PLATE 31

BLACK	WHITE
35. R 15.	**36.** S 16.
37. P 13.	**38.** P 12.
39. N 13.	**40.** O 13.
41. O 14.	**42.** O 12.
43. L 13.	**44.** R 6.
45. D 7.	

VIII

No Handicap

Plate 32

BLACK	WHITE
1. C 4.	**2.** C 16.
3. Q 3.	**4.** R 5.
5. R 9.	**6.** O 5.
7. N 3.	**8.** R 12.
9. P 9.	**10.** Q 16.
11. R 4.	**12.** Q 5.
13. P 4.	**14.** P 5.
15. M 4.	**16.** M 7.
17. O 17.	**18.** E 16.
19. C 10.	**20.** E 3.
21. D 5.	**22.** K 17.
23. R 17.	**24.** Q 17.
25. R 16.	**26.** Q 15.
27. Q 18.	**28.** P 18.
29. R 18.	**30.** P 17.
31. R 14.	**32.** Q 14.
33. R 13.	**34.** Q 13.
35. S 12.	**36.** K 15.
37. C 13.	**38.** E 13.
39. Q 12.	**40.** R 15.
41. S 15.	**42.** S 16.
43. S 14.	**44.** P 12.

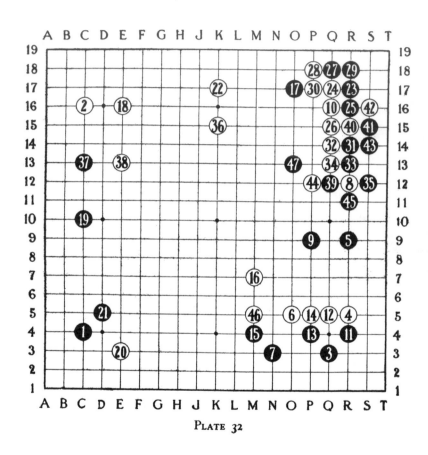

PLATE 32

BLACK	WHITE
45. R 11. Takes.	**46.** M 5. This move is necessary because Black's position above it has become strong.

47. O 13. The continuation would now be either 48 P 13, 49 O 15, or 48 O 15, 49 P 13.

IX

No Handicap

Plate 33

BLACK	WHITE
1. C 4.	**2.** Q 3.
3. D 17.	**4.** E 3.
5. R 16.	**6.** C 15.
7. D 5.	**8.** P 17.
9. F 4.	**10.** C 11. White cannot play 10 at G 3 because Black would then occupy C 11.
11. F 3.	**12.** K 3.
13. R 5.	**14.** O 4.
15. F 16.	**16.** H 17.
17. C 13.	**18.** C 8. Abandoning the stone at C 15.
19. C 16.	**20.** R 13.
21. Q 15.	**22.** N 16.
23. Q 17.	**24.** P 18.
25. R 9. If 25 were played at Q 8, 26 R 8 would be the result.	**26.** P 14.
27. O 16.	**28.** O 15.
29. P 16.	**30.** N 17.
31. Q 18.	**32.** R 7.

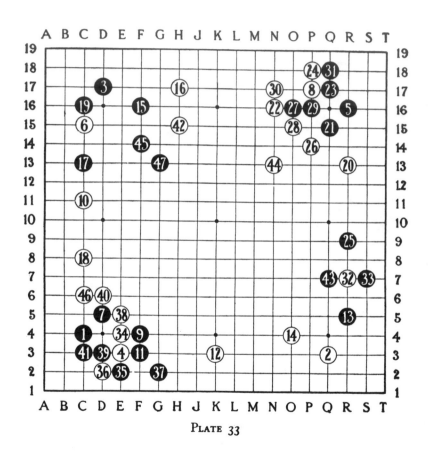

PLATE 33

BLACK

33. S 7. This move insures a connection between the stones at R 5 and R 9.

WHITE

34. E 4. This move rescues No. 4.

BLACK	WHITE
35. E 2.	**36.** D 2.
37. G 2.	**38.** E 5.
39. D 3.	**40.** D 6.
41. C 3.	**42.** H 15.
43. Q 7.	**44.** N 13. This prevents Black from cutting at N 15 and Q 13.
45. F 14.	**46.** C 6.
47. G 13.	

X

No Handicap

Plate 34

BLACK	WHITE
1. C 4.	**2.** Q 3.
3. D 17.	**4.** E 3.
5. R 16.	**6.** C 15.
7. D 5.	**8.** F 16.
9. D 15.	**10.** D 16.
11. E 16.	**12.** C 16.
13. E 17.	**14.** E 15.
15. D 14.	**16.** C 17.
17. F 17.	**18.** G 16.
19. H 18. This move is much better than G 17.	**20.** C 14.
21. E 14.	**22.** F 15.
23. F 14.	**24.** H 16.
25. J 17.	**26.** G 18.
27. F 18.	**28.** G 14.
29. E 12.	**30.** C 11.

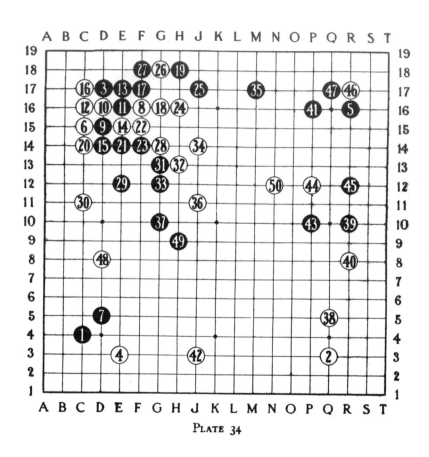

PLATE 34

BLACK	WHITE
31. G 13.	**32.** H 13
33. G 12. H 14 would be bad.	**34** J 14.
35. M 17.	**36.** J 11
37. G 10.	**38.** Q 5.
39. R 10.	**40.** R 8.
41. P 16.	**42.** J 3.
43. P 10.	**44.** P 12.
45. R 12.	**46.** R 17. A sacrifice.
47. Q 17.	**48.** D 8.
49. H 9.	**50.** N 12.

VII

THE END GAME

A work on the game of Go would not be complete without a chapter especially devoted to the subject of the end game.

On the average a game of Go consists of about two hundred and fifty moves, and we might say that about twenty of these moves belong to the opening, about one hundred and fifty to the main part of the game, and the remaining eighty to the end game. The moves which may be regarded as belonging to the end game are those which connect the various groups of stones with the margin, and which fill up the space between the opposing groups of stones. Of course, there is no sharp distinction between the main game and the end game. Long before the main game is finished moves occur which bear the characteristics of end game play, and as the game progresses moves of this kind become more and more frequent, until at last all of the moves are strictly part of the end game.

Toward the end of the game it becomes possible to calculate the value of a move with greater accuracy than in the middle of the game, and in many cases the number of points which may be gained by a certain move may be ascertained with absolute accuracy. Therefore, when the main game is nearing completion, the players survey the board in order to locate the most advantageous end plays; that is to say, positions where they can gain the greatest number of "Me." In calculating the value of an end position, a player must carefully consider whether on its completion he will retain or lose the "Sente." It is an advantage to retain the "Sente," and it is generally good play to choose an end position where the "Sente" is retained, in preference to an end position where it is lost, even if the latter would gain a few more "Me."

The player holding the "Sente" would, therefore, complete in rotation those end positions which allowed him to retain it, commencing, of course, with those involving the greatest number of "Me." He would at last come to a point, however, where it would be more advantageous to play some end position which gained for him quite a number of points, although on its completion the "Sente" would be lost. His adversary, thereupon gaining the "Sente," would, in turn, play his series of end positions until it became advantageous for him to relinquish it. By this process the value of the contested end positions would become smaller and smaller, until at last there would remain only the filling of isolated, vacant intersections between the opposing lines, the occupation of which results in no advantage for either player. These moves are called "Dame," as we have already seen.

This is the general scheme of an end game, but, of course, in actual play there would be many departures therefrom. Sometimes an advantage can be gained by making an unsound though dangerous move, in the hope that the adversary may make some error in replying thereto. Then again, in playing against a player who lacks initiative, it is not so necessary to consider the certainty of retaining the "Sente" as when opposed by a more aggressive adversary.

Frequently also the players differ in their estimate of the value of the various end positions, and do not, therefore, respond to each other's attacks. In this way the possession of the "Sente" generally changes more frequently during the end game than is logically necessary.

The process of connecting the various groups with the edge of the board gives rise to end positions in which there is more or less similarity in all games, and most of the illustrations which are now given are examples of this class. The end positions which occur in the middle of the board may vary so much in every game that it is practically impossible to give typical illustrations of them.

Of course, in an introductory work of this character it is not practicable to give a great many examples of end positions, and I have prepared only twelve, which are selected from the work of Inouye Hoshin, and which are annotated so that the reasons for the moves may be understood by beginners. The number of "Me" gained in each case is stated, and also whether the "Sente" is lost or retained. To these twelve examples I have added eight positions from Korschelt's work.

I

Plate 35 (A)

The following stones are on the board: White, S 15, R 14, P 14, L 17; Black, R 16, Q 16, N 15, N 17.

If White has the "Sente," he gains eight "Me," counting together what he wins and Black loses.

WHITE	BLACK
1. S 17. This is White's only good move; S 16 does not take ad-	2. S 16. If Black had had the move or "Sente," he could have

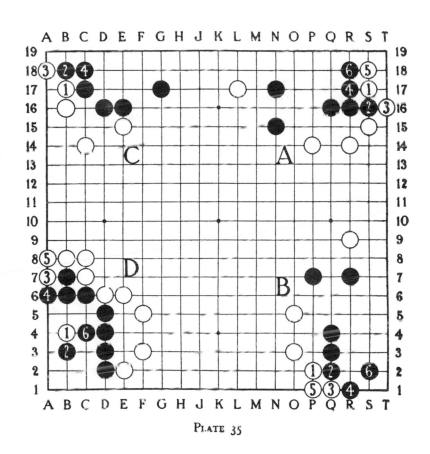

PLATE 35

WHITE	BLACK
vantage of the opportunity, and he cannot risk S 18.	avoided White's invasion by playing here.
3. T 16. An instance of "Watari."	**4.** R 17.
5. S 18. White cannot venture to play at R 18.	**6.** R 18. If Black neglects this, White would jump to Q 18.

White retains the "Sente."

II

Plate 35 (*B*)

The following stones are on the board: White, R 9, O 5, O 3; Black, P 7, Q 3, Q 4, R 7.

If White has the first move, it makes a difference of six "Me."

WHITE	BLACK
1. P 2.	**2.** Q 2.
3. Q 1.	**4.** R 1.
5. P 1.	**6.** S 2. Black cannot neglect this move.

White retains the "Sente."

If Black had had the first move, the play would have been as follows:

BLACK	WHITE
1. P 2.	**2.** O 2.
3. O 1.	**4.** N 1.
5. P 1.	**6.** M 2.

And Black has the "Sente."

III

Plate 35 (C)

The following stones are on the board: White, B 16, C 14, E 15; Black, C 17, D 16, E 16, G 17.

If White has the move, it makes a difference of seven "Me."

WHITE	BLACK
1. B 17. White dare not go to B 18 because he would be cut off eventually at B 15.	**2.** B 18.
3. A 18.	**4.** C 18.

White retains the "Sente."

IV

Plate 35 (D)

The following stones are on the board: White, B 8, C 7, C 8, D 6, E 2, E 6, F 3, F 5; Black, B 6, B 7, C 6, D 2, 3, 4, 5.

If White has the move, it makes a difference of four "Me."

WHITE	BLACK
1. B 4. This stone is sacrificed, but there is no loss because it is so threatening that Black must play twice in order to make his position secure, meanwhile White advances on line A.	**2.** B 3. Black's best move because it defends the connection at C 5, and also prevents White from trying to connect at D 1.
3. A 7. White gains one "Me" by this move.	**4.** A 6.

5. A 8.

6. C 4. Necessary because the connection at C 5 is now in immediate danger, but Black thereby fills up another of his "Me," and White retains the "Sente."

V

Plate 36 (A)

The following stones are on the board: White, M 16, M 17, M 18, N 16, O 15, P 14, R 14; Black, N 17, N 18, O 16, P 16, Q 16, R 16.

If White has the "Sente," it makes a difference of six "Me."

WHITE

BLACK

1. N 19.

2. O 18. Black cannot stop the invasion at O 19, as White would then play at O 18 and kill the black stones on line N.

3. O 19. White pushes his invasion farther.

4. P 19. Black can now arrest the advance.

5. M 19.

6. P 18.

White retains the "Sente."

VI

Plate 36 (B)

The following stones are on the board: Black, M 2, M 3, N 3, N 4, O 4, Q 4, R 4, S 4; White, L 3, N 2, O 2, O 3, P 3, R 2, S 3, R 6.

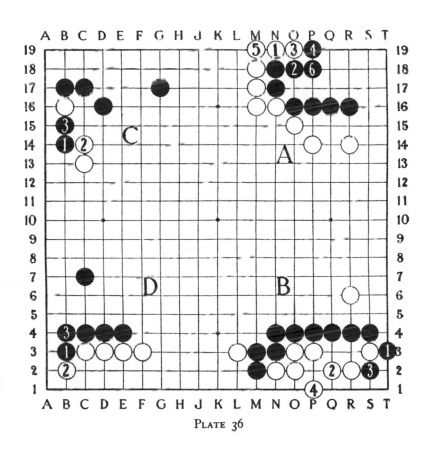

PLATE 36

Black has the "Sente" and gains nine "Me."

BLACK	WHITE
1. T 3.	**2.** Q 2. The obvious answer is at T 2, but if White plays there, Black replies at Q 2 and White loses all his stones unless he can win by "Ko." He plays at Q 2 in order to form the necessary two "Me."
3. S 2. Black proceeds with his invasion.	**4.** P 1. If White tries to save his stone by playing at R 3, Black replies at P 1, and the white group is dead.

Black retains the "Sente."

VII

Plate 36 (*C*)

The following stones are on the board: Black, B 17, C 17, D 16, G 17; White, B 16, C 13.

BLACK	WHITE
1. B 14. This move is really "Go te"; that is to say, White is not forced to reply to it, but it is very advantageous for Black, as it effectively separates White's two stones.	**2.** C 14. C 15 is not so good.
3. B 15. The white stone at B 16 is now hopeless.	

Black has given up the "Sente," but has gained considerable ground.

VIII

Plate 36 (D)

The following stones are on the board: Black, C 4, D 4, E 4, C 7; White, C 3, D 3, E 3, F 3.

Black has the move.

BLACK	WHITE
1. B 3.	2. B 2.
3. B 4.	

These moves seem obvious, but the importance of Black's opportunity is likely to be underestimated; Black gains about eleven "Me" by this play. If the opposing lines extend one space nearer the edge of the board, the territory gained by a similar attack is not nearly so great.

IX

Plate 37 (A)

The following stones are on the board: White, M 16, N 16, N 18, O 17, P 18, Q 17, 18; Black, N 15, O 15, 16, P 16, 17, Q 16, R 12, R 17.

White has the move.

WHITE	BLACK
1. S 17.	2. S 16.
3. R 18.	4. R 16.
5. T 18.	

White has given up the "Sente," but these moves make a difference in his favor of about fourteen "Me."

X

Plate 37 (*B*)

The following stones are on the board: White, M 3, O 3, P 2, Q 3, R 2; Black, N 4, O 4, Q 5, R 3, R 4.

White has the move.

WHITE	BLACK
1. S 2.	

This move is really "Go te," but if Black neglects to answer it, White can then jump to T 5. This jump is called by a special name "O zaru," or the "big monkey," and would gain about eight "Me." for White

XI

Plate 37 (*C*)

The following stones are on the board: White, C 15, D 15, E 15, 16; Black, C 16, D 16, E 17, 18, F 16, G 17.

White has the move.

WHITE	BLACK
1. B 16.	2. B 17.
3. B 15.	

White has given up the "Sente" and has gained somewhat, but if Black now neglects to defend and plays elsewhere, White can jump to B 18, and gain about seventeen "Me" altogether.

XII

Plate 37 (*D*)

The following stones are on the board: White, B 8, C 7, 11, D 5, 6, 7, E 6; Black, B 7, C 5, 6, D 3, 4, E 4, 5.

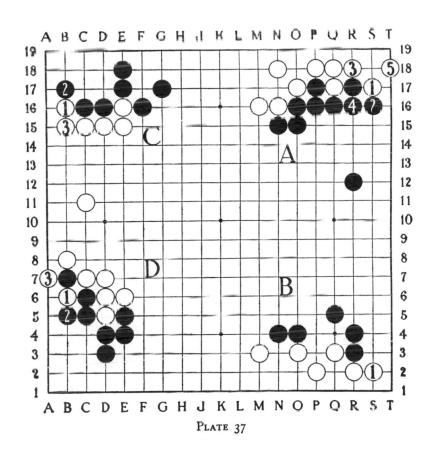

White has the move.

WHITE	BLACK
1. B 6.	**2.** B 5.
3. A 7. Takes.	

White has given up the "Sente," but this method of play gains about fourteen "Me," as it is now no longer necessary to protect the connection at C 8.

We will now insert two plates from Korschelt's book. The notes at the foot of the illustrations are his.

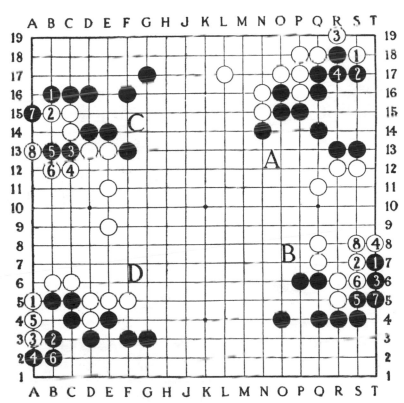

A WORTH SIX "ME" (S 17, 18, 19 T 17, 18, 19); SENTE IS RE-
   TAINED
B WORTH FIVE "ME"; SENTE IS RETAINED
C WORTH THIRTEEN "ME"; SENTE IS RETAINED
D WORTH EIGHT "ME"; SENTE IS RETAINED

PLATE 38

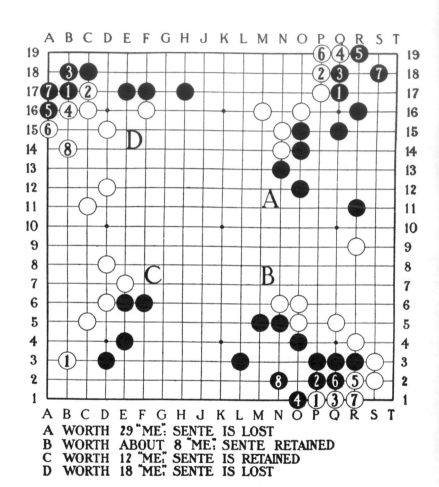

A WORTH 29 "ME": SENTE IS LOST
B WORTH ABOUT 8 "ME": SENTE RETAINED
C WORTH 12 "ME": SENTE IS RETAINED
D WORTH 18 "ME": SENTE IS LOST

PLATE 39

VIII

PROBLEMS

AFTER the student has become familiar with the rules and the methods of play, and perhaps has played a few games either with another beginner or with a Japanese master, the impression left on the mind is likely to be that the game is too vague, and that there is too wide a latitude of choice of positions where stones may be placed. This impression might be corrected by the study of illustrative games, or of "Joseki" and end positions, but such a course is rather dry and uninteresting, and, in the opinion of the author, by far the best way of attaining a correct idea of the game is by means of problems.

Many of us are familiar with Chess problems, and I think Chess players will agree that they benefit the student of Chess very little, because the assumed positions are not such as arise frequently in actual play. The opposite is the case in regard to Go problems. These are for the most part taken from actual games, and the typical problem is a situation that is quite likely to arise in actual play, and some of them are positions that occur again and again.

If the student of the game will set up these positions from the text and attempt to solve them, preferably with the aid and encouragement of some friend, he will find that the task is an interesting one, and he will be impressed by the great accuracy which is necessary in attacking and defending difficult positions.

With the knowledge obtained in this way, he will be

able to judge with far greater skill what to do when a position is threatened in actual play. He will be able to distinguish whether the danger is real, and whether it is, therefore, necessary to reply to his adversary's attack, or whether he can afford to ignore it and assume the "Sente" in some other part of the board. He will also be able to perceive when an adversary's group is vulnerable so that it will be profitable to attack it.

The collection of problems which I have given in this book are rearranged from Korschelt's work, and they were in turn taken by him from a Japanese treatise called "Go Kiyo Shiyu Miyo." Necessarily the collection here given is a very small one, but if any reader of this book becomes so much interested in the game that he desires to study other examples, he will doubtless find some Japanese acquaintance who can supply him with further material, as the Japanese literature of the game contains large collections.

The most important kind of problems are those in which the question is how to kill an adversary's group, or how to save one's own group when threatened. It is also often very important to know how a connection between two groups can be forced.

For greater clearness these problems are arranged under seven heads; to wit,

1. SAVING THREATENED GROUPS.
2. KILLING GROUPS.
3. PLAYING FOR "KO."
    The advantage gained by this operation is not apparent in the group itself, but depends upon which player has the larger threatened group elsewhere.
4. RECIPROCAL ATTACKS OR "SEMEAI."

This is a combination of the first two kinds of problems, and it only differs from them in that both players have comparatively strong groups which are so intertwined that both cannot live, and the question is, which can kill the other first.

5. CONNECTING GROUPS.

The problem here is to force a connection between a small group having insufficient "Me" and some larger group.

6. "OI OTOSHI."

This really means a "robber's attack." It arises where a group is apparently engulfed by the opponent, and when, by adding further stones to it which the opponent must take, the threatened player can force his opponent to abandon a part of his surrounding chain in order not to sustain greater losses. The attack is so sudden and unexpected that the Japanese compare it to the methods of a highwayman. It is an example of the finest play in the game.

7. CUTTING.

This is another method of escape, and the problem is to cut off and kill part of the adversary's surrounding chain.

In the following examples the side having the first move is given in italics.

I. SAVING THREATENED GROUPS

1. (Plate 40, A) *White*, Q 18, R 18, S 16, 17, 18.
  Black, O 17, P 18, Q 17, R 15, 17, S 15.
2. (Plate 40, B) White, O 3, Q 3, 4, R 3, 5, S 5.
  Black, R 2, 4, S 3, 4.
3. (Plate 40, C) White, A 14, B 11, 13, C 13, 14, 15, 17, D 17, 18, E 16, F 17.
  Black, A 13, B 14, 15, 17, 18, C 16, 18.

4. (Plate 40, D) *White*, B 3, C 3, D 2, E 2.
Black, B 4, C 4, D 3, E 3, F 2, G 3.

5. White, B 5, C 4, D 5, E 2, 3, 4, G 2.
Black, B 3, 4, D 2, 3, E 1.

6. *White*, B 12, 13, 15, 16, C 13, 15, D 13, 14.
Black, A 16, B 11, 17, C 10, 12, 16, D 12, 15, 16, E 13, 14.

7. White, M 16, 17, N 16, O 15, 17, P 14, 17, Q 18, R 14, S 15.
Black, N 17, O 16, P 16, Q 16, R 16, S 16, 18 .

8. *White*, O 1, P 2, Q 2, 3, R 3, S 3, 4.
Black, N 2, O 2, P 1, 3, 4, Q 4, R 4, 6, S 5, T 4.

9. White, A 4, B 5, 6, C 4, D 5, E 2, 3, 4.
Black, A 5, B 3, 4, C 3, D 2, 3.

10. *White*, B 15, 16, C 17, 18, D 18.
Black, A 15, B 14, C 14, 15, 16, D 17, E 17, 18.

11. White, L 18, M 16, 17, N 14, 18, O 13, 19, P 18, Q 12, 13, 17, 18, R 12,
14, 18, S 14, 17, 19.
Black, N 17, O 15, 17, 18, P 14, 17, Q 14, 15, 16, R 13, 16, 17, S 13,
18.

12. *White*, Q 3, R 2, 3, S 3.
Black, P 2, 3, 5, Q 2, 4, R 5, 7.

13. *White*, B 2, C 3, D 1, 3, E 2.
Black, B 4, C 5, D 4, E 3, 4, F 1, 2, G 3.

14. White, A 16, B 15, C 15, 16, D 17, E 17, F 18, G 18.
Black, B 16, 17, C 17, D 18, E 18, F 19.

15. *White*, Q 15, R 14, 15, 16, S 17.
Black, P 15, 17, Q 13, 14, 16, R 11, 12, 17, 18.

16. *White*, R 3, 4, 5, S 2.
Black, O 3, P 3, Q 4, 6, R 6, S 6, T 3.

17. White, B 4, C 3, 4, 5, E 4, F 2, 3, H 2.
Black, B 3, C 2, D 3, E 2, F 1.

18. *White*, C 13, 15, 16, 17, E 14, 15, 16.
Black, B 14, 15, C 12, 14, D 13, 17, E 12, 17, F 15, 16, G 13.

19. White, M 17, N 18, O 17, 19, P 15, 17, R 14, 16, S 16.
Black, O 18, P 18, Q 16, 17, R 17, S 17.

20. White, P 2, 3, 6, Q 2, 4, R 2, 4, 6, 7.
Black, Q 3, R 1, 3, 9, S 2, 4, 5.

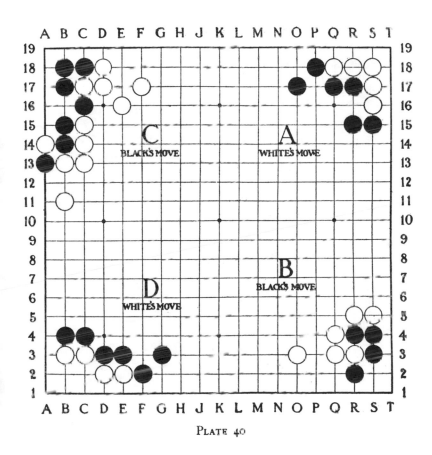

PLATE 40

21. White, B 13, 14, 16, C 13, D 13, 14, 15, 18, E 16, 17.
    Black, B 15, C 14, 15, 17, 18, D 16.
22. *White*, C 7, D 3, 5, 6, E 2, 3, 7, F 5.
    Black, C 2, 4, 5, 6, 9, 10, D 2, E 8, F 2, 8, G 3, 5, 6, J 3.
23. White, O 2, 3, 4, 6, Q 4, R 4, 6, S 5, T 4.
    Black, P 2, 3, R 3, S 3, 4.
24. *White*, Q 17, R 16, 17, S 18.
    Black, N 17, O 17, P 16, Q 16, R 15, S 16, 17.

II. KILLING GROUPS

1. (Plate 41, A) *White*, O 17, P 18, Q 14, 15, 16, 17, R 13, S 13, 14, 15.
   Black, Q 18, R 14, 15, 16, 17, 18, S 16, T 15.
2. (Plate 41, B) White, P 5, Q 3, R 2, 5, S 5, 6.
   Black, O 2, P 3, 4, 6, Q 2, 5, R 6, 7, S 8.
3. (Plate 41, C) White, B 15, 18, C 16, 17.
   Black, B 14, C 14, D 15. 16, 17, 18.
4. (Plate 41, *D*) *White*, B 4, C 3, 4, E 1, 3, F 2, 4, G 2.
   Black, A 3, B 2, 3, C 2, D 2, E 2, F 1.
5. *White*, B 4, C 4, D 3, E 3, F 2, G 3.
   Black, A 3, B 3, C 2, D 2, E 2.
6. White, B 16, C 10, D 13, 15, 16, 17.
   Black, B 14, C 12, 15, D 18, E 12, F 14, 15, 17, G 17.
7. *White*, P 17, 18, Q 15, 16, R 13, 15.
   Black, Q 17, 18, R 16, S 16.
8. White, Q 1, R 2, 3, 5, S 5.
   Black, O 2, Q 2, 3, 4, 5, 6, R 7, S 7.
9. *White*, B 5, C 5, 8, D 5, E 2, 4, F 2, 3, 4.
   Black, B 4, C 4, D 2, 3, E 3.
10. White, B 15, C 15, 17, 18.
    Black, B 14, C 12, 14, D 15, 16, 17, F 17.
11. *White*, M 16, O 15, 16, 18, P 18, Q 14, R 12, 15, 18, S 16.
    Black, L 16, P 16, 17, Q 16, 18, S 17, 18.
12. White, Q 2, R 2, S 3, 4, 5.
    Black, P 2, 3, Q 3, R 4, 5, 7, S 6.
13. *White*, B 4, C 4, 6, D 4, E 3, F 3, G 2, H 3.
    Black, B 3, C 3, D 3, E 2, F 2.

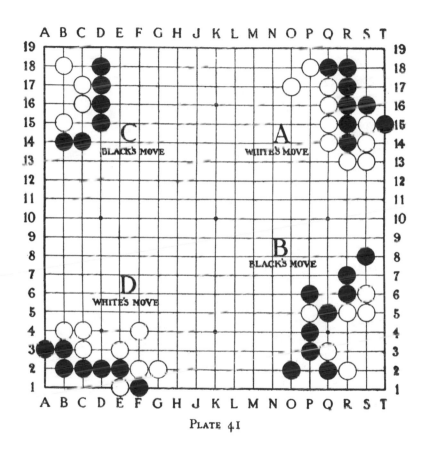

PLATE 41

14. White, C 17, 18, E 16, 17, F 15, G 16, H 16, 17, K 16.
   Black, B 17, 18, C 16, D 14, 16, 17, E 13, 15, G 14, 15, 17, J 14, 15,
   K, 17, L 16.
15. *White*, N 17, P 16, 17, 18, Q 15, R 13, 15, S 14.
   Black, Q 16, 17, 18, R 16, S 15.
16. White, P 2, Q 2, R 3.
   Black, N 3, O 3, Q 3, 4, R 5.
17. White, B 16, 17, C 17, D 18, 19.
   Black, C 12, 14, 16, D 16, 17, E 18, F 17.
18. *White*, H 3, K 3, 4, M 3, N 4, O 2, P 3, 4, Q 6, R 5, S 1, 4.
   Black, P 1, 2, Q 3, R 2, 3, S 3.
19. *White*, M 17, O 16, 17, P 15, R 13, 15, S 15, 16.
   Black, P 16, Q 16, 18, R 16, S 17.

III. Playing for "Ko"

1. (Plate 42, A) White, O 16, P 17, 18, Q 16, R 14, 16, S 15.
   Black, Q 17, 18, R 17, S 16.
2. (Plate 42, B) White, O 4, 5, P 2, 3, 6, R 2, 6, 7, S 3, 5.
   Black, L 3, N 3, O 3, P 4, Q 4, R 4, 9, S 4, 7, T 4.
3. (Plate 42, C) *White*, B 16, 17, C 18.
   Black, C 13, 15, 16, 17, D 18, E 17.
4. (Plate 42, D) White, B 4, C 4, D 4, E 3, 4, F 2, G 4.
   Black, C 2, 3, D 3, E 2.
5. *White*, B 4, C 4, D 3, E 3, F 2, 3.
   Black, B 3, C 1, 3, D 2, E 2.
6. *White*, C 15, 16, 17, D 18.
   Black, B 14, C 12, 14, D 15, 16, 17, E 18, F 17.
7. *White*, P 17, 18, Q 17, R 15, 16, S 15.
   Black, Q 18, R 17, 19, S 16, 17.
8. *White*, Q 3, R 3, S 4.
   Black, O 3, P 3, Q 4, R 4, 6, S 5.
9. *White*, B 5, C 4, 5, E 4, F 4, H 2, 4, 5, J 3.
   Black, B 3, 4, D 3, E 3, F 3, G 3.
10. *White*, B 15, 16, C 17, 18, D 19.
   Black, B 14, 18, C 14, 15, D 16, 18, E 18, F 16.

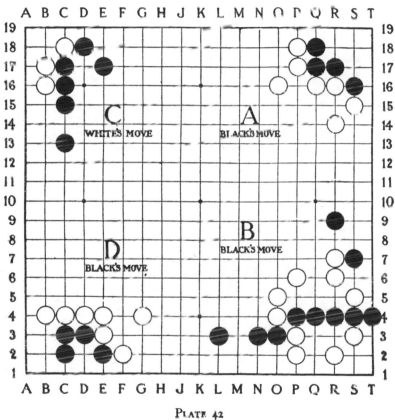

PLATE 42

11. White, N 17, O 18, P 16, 17, Q 16, R 16, S 16.
   Black, P 18, Q 17, R 17, S 17.
12. *White*, P 2, Q 2, R 3, 4, S 2.
   Black, M 3, O 3, P 3, Q 5, R 5, S 3, 4, T 2.
13. White, A 2, B 3, 4, C 5, D 4, 5, F 4, G 2, 3.
   Black, B 2, C 3, 4, D 3, E 3, F 2.
14. *White*, C 15, 16, 17, D 16.
   Black, C 14, D 14, 15, 17, 18, E 16, F 17.
15. White, N 17, O 18, P 16, 17, Q 15, R 15, S 16.
   Black, P 18, Q 16, 17, S 17.
16. *White*, R 2, 4, S 3.
   Black, O 3, P 4, Q 2, 4, R 5, 6, S 4.

IV. Reciprocal Attacks (" Semeai ")

1. (Plate 43, A) *White*, N 17, P 17, Q 17, R 17, S 18.
   Black, Q 18, R 14, 16, 18, S 16, 17.
2. (Plate 43, B) White, O 3, P 2, Q 2, R 3, S 3, 5.
   Black, Q 3, 4, R 2, 6, S 2, 7.
3. (Plate 43, C) White, B 15, 16, C 15, 17, 18, D 17, E 18.
   Black, B 17, C 16, D 16, 18, E 16, 17, F 18.
4. (Plate 43, D) *White*, B 2, 3, 4, C 5, D 3, 4, 6, F 3, G 2, 3.
   Black, B 5, 6, C 2, 3, 4, 7, D 2, E 2. F 2.
5. *White*, B 3, C 2, 3, 4, D 4, E 3, F 3, G 2, 3.
   Black, A 3, 5, B 4, 6, C 5, D 2, 3, 5, E 2, 4, 5, F 2.
6. White, B 14, 15, 16, 19, C 15, 17, 18, D 18, E 17, F 17.
   Black, B 13, 17, 18, C 13, 14, 16, D 15, 16, 17, E 14.
7. *White*, N 17, O 17, Q 16, 17, R 18, S 18.
   Black, P 18, Q 15, 18, R 15, 17, S 17.
8. White, P 2, 4, Q 2, 6, R 3, 7, S 3, 6.
   Black, N 3, O 2, 3, P 3, Q 3, R 4, 5, S 4.
9. *White*, A 4, B 5, C 5, 7, D 2, 3, 5, E 3, 4.
   Black, B 3, 4, C 2, 4, D 4, 6, E 5, 6, F 2, 4, G 3.
10. White, B 13, 14, 15, C 15, 18, D 16, 17, 18.
   Black, B 12, 16, C 12, 13, 14, 16, 17, D 15, E 15.
11. White, O 2, 4, P 2, 4, Q 2, 3, 5, R 5, 7, S 4.
   Black, M 3, N 2, 3, O 3, P 3, Q 4, R 3, 4.

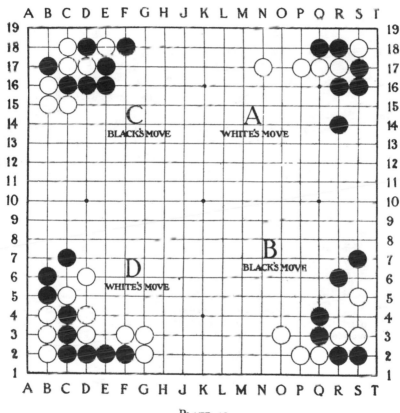

PLATE 43

12. *White*, Q 11, 12, 13, R 11, 14, 15, S 16, T 14.
Black, Q 14, 15, R 12, 13, 16, 17, 18, S 11, 13.

V. CONNECTING GROUPS

1. (Plate 44, A) White, K 14, 16, 18, L 18, M 13, N 13, 15, O 16, P 14, 17.

    Black, M 16, 18, N 14, 17, Q 14, 15, 16, R 17.

2. (Plate 44, B) *White*, N 5, O 4, 6, P 4, Q 3, 8, R 3, 8, S 3, 4, 7, 9.
    Black, N 6, P 5, 6, 8, 9, R 4, 6, 7, 10, 11, S 5.

3. (Plate 44, C) White, C 11, 12, 13, 14, 18, D 14, 17, E 18, G 17.
    Black, B 10, C 9, 16, 17, D 10, 13, 15, E 11, 14, F 13, 16.

4. (Plate 44, D) *White*, C 2, 3, 5, 6, E 7, G 3, 5, H 3, 5.
    Black, D 3, 5, E 5, F 3, 6, G 6, J 4, 7, K 3, 6.

5. White, A 2, B 2, 5, C 6, D 3, E 5, 7, F 5, G 2, 3.
Black, C 1, 2, 3, 4, D 4, G 5, H 2, 3, 4.

6. *White*, B 13, 17, C 13, 17, D 13, 16, 17, E 17, F 17.
Black, B 15, C 10, 14, 16, D 11, E 14, 16, F 12, 14.

7. *White*, M 2, 3, P 2, 3, R 2, 3, 4, S 5, 6.
Black, N 4, P 4, Q 2, 3, 4, 6, R 5, S 2, 3.

8. White, M 13, 15, N 11, O 10, 15, P 13, Q 9, 14, R 10, 15, S 12, 16.
Black, O 12, 17, P 12, Q 16, R 11, 12, 13, 17, S 13, 17.

9 White, B 2, 3, C 2, 4, D 6, F 4, 7, G 3, 5, H 3, 5, J 6, K 5, L 4.
Black, C 3, D 2, 3, E 3, 5, F 3, G 4, J 4, 5, K 4, L 3, M 3.

10. White, C 12, 17, D 9, 14, 18, E 10, 12, 13, 17, F 17, G 15, H 12, 14.
Black, C 8, 9, 14, 15, 16, D 10, E 15, 16, F 13, 14.

11. *White*, H 17, J 17, K 17, N 15, O 15, 17, P 17.
Black, J 16, K 14, 16, M 14, 16, N 16, O 13, Q 14, 17, R 16.

12. *White*, Q 8, 9, R 3, 4, 5, 10, 11, 12, S 2.
Black, P 3, 5, 7, 8, 9, Q 2, 5, 10, R 2, 7, S 1.

VI. "OI OTOSHI"

1. (Plate 45, A) *White*, P 18, Q 15, 16, 17, R 17, 18, S 17.
    Black, O 17, 18, P 14, 16, Q 14, R 14, 16, S 16, 18, T 17.

2. (Plate 45, B) White, N 5, O 4, P 3, 4, 6, Q 2, R 2, 7, S 3, 4, 6, T 5.
    Black, M 4, N 2, 4, O 3, P 1, 2, Q 3, 5, R 3, 5, S 5.

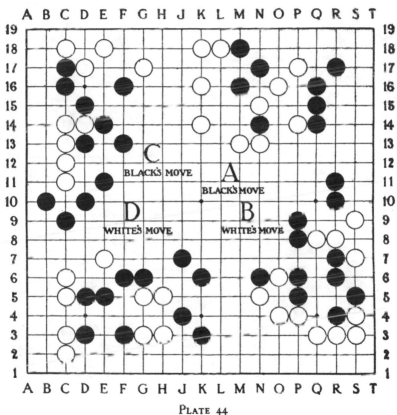

C
BLACK'S MOVE

A
BLACK'S MOVE

D
WHITE'S MOVE

B
WHITE'S MOVE

PLATE 44

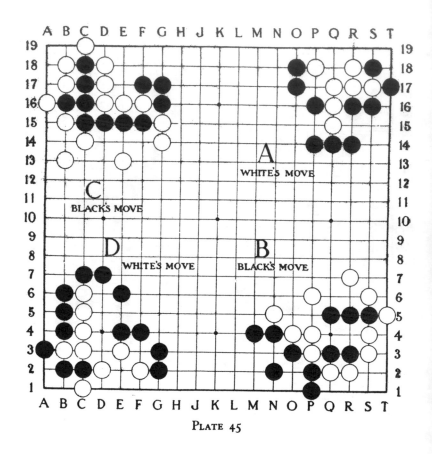

PLATE 45

3. (Plate 45, C) White, A 16, B 13, 15, 17, 18, C 14, 19, D 16, 17, 18, E 13, 16, F 16, G 14, 15.

Black, B 16, C 15, 16, 17, 18, D 15, E 15, F 15, 17, G 16, 17.

4. (Plate 45, D) White, B 3, C 1, 3, 4, 5, 6, D 2, E 3, F 2.

Black, A 3, B 2, 4, 5, 6, C 2, 7, D 7, E 4, 6, F 4, G 2, 3.

5. White, A 3, B 4, C 4, D 3, 4, F 3, 3, 4.

Black, B 3, C 3, 5, 6, D 2, E 2, 6, F 1, G 2, 4, 5, H 3.

6. White, A 18, B 15, 17, C 14, 18, D 14, 19, E 14, 18, F 15, 18, G 19, H 16, 17, 18.

Black, A 16, B 16, 18, C 16, D 15, 17, 18, E 17, F 17, G 17, 18.

7. White, P 5, 6, Q 3, 4, 9, R 3, 9, S 4, 5, 7, 8, T 6.

Black, N 4, P 2, 3, 4, Q 5, R 4, 5, 6, 7, 8, S 6.

8. White, Q 16, 17, 18, R 13, 14, 15, 16, 18, S 16.

Black, O 17, P 12, 15, 18, Q 13, 15, R 12, 17; S 13, 14, 15, 17, 18, T 16.

9. White, A 3, 4, B 4, 6, C 2, 3, 5, D 1, 3, E 3, F 3, G 3, H 3, J 2, 3.

Black, B 1, 2, 3, C 1, 4, D 2, 4, E 2, 4, F 2, 5, G 2, H 2, 5, J 1, K 3, 3, 4.

10. White, A 9, 12, B 8, 10, 11, 13, 14, 16, 17, C 8, 15, D 9, 15, E 11, 13, 14.

Black, A 18, B 9, 12, 18, C 9, 10, 11, 12, 13, 14, 17, D 14, 17, E 15, 16.

11. White, H 17, J 15, 18, L 14, 15, M 14, N 15, 16, 17, O 17, 18, P 17, Q 17.

Black, K 17, L 16, M 15, 16, 18, N 14, 18, O 14, 19, P 18, Q 15, 18, R 16, 17.

12. White, O 4, 6, P 2, 3, 8, Q 9, R 4, 5, 6, 9, S 3, 4, 7, 9, T 7, 8.

Black, Q 3, 4, 5, 6, 7, R 3, 7, 8, S 2, 6, 8, T 2.

VII. CUTTING

1. (Plate 46, A) White, C 15, D 17, 18, E 15, 17, G 18, H 18, J 13, K 13, 14, 15, 16, 17, 18.

Black, E 18, F 12, 17, 18, G 13, 15, 17, H 12, J 11, 14, L 12, 16, 18, M 14, 16, N 18.

2. (Plate 46, B) White, J 3, K 5, 6, L 3, 4, 7, P 3, 5, 7, Q 2, 3, 9, R 6.

Black, L 5, 8, M 3, 8, N 3, 5, 7, O 3, 8, P 2.

3. White, C 15, D 18, E 13, 15, 16, 17, H 18, J 12, 15, 17, K 13, 14, 15, 17.

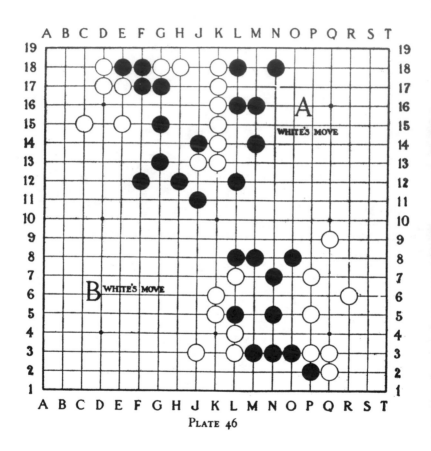

PLATE 46

Black, E 18, F 12, 13, 17, 18, G 15, 17, H 12, 13, J 11, 14, L 12, 16, 17, M 14.

4. White, H 5, 7, 9, 10, J 3, K 3, 5, 7, 9, L 2, 3, M 2, 9, O 4, 6, 7, 8, Q 3, R 3.

Black, G 5, 6, 7, 9, H 3, 4, 8, J 2, M 3, 5, 7, N 2, 3, 5, 7, P 2, Q 2.

SOLUTIONS TO PROBLEMS

I. SAVING THREATENED GROUPS

1. T 19.
2. T 2, S 1, T 4, Q 2, R 1.
3. A 18, A 16, B 16.
4. B 2, C 1, B 1, D 1, C 2.
5. A 2, B 1, A 4 or A 2, A 4, B 1.
6. C 17, C 18, D 17, E 17, B 18, D 18, A 18, B 19, A 12, A 14, B 14.
7. O 18, N 18, Q 17, R 18, P 18, N 17, R 17, O 19, R 19, P 19, T 17 or O 18, P 18, R 18, or O 18, R 18, P 18.
8. S 2, R 1, S 1.
9. B 1, A 2, B 2.
10. A 17, B 19, B 18, A 14, C 19, A 16, A 19, B 17, B 16.
11. T 16, T 18, T 14 or T 16, S 12, T 18.
12. S 5, S 6, T 5.
13. C 1.
14. B 19.
15. S 18, S 19, S 13, T 18, S 15, T 17, T 14 or S 18, S 13, T 16.
16. S 5, T 5, T 4, S 4, T 2, T 6, Q 2, or S 5, T 5, T 4, S 4, T 2, Q 2, S 3, T 4, T 6, T 4, T 5, S 1, S 8.
17. A 3, B 1, B 2, E 3, A 1, A 2, C 1.
18. F 17, G 17, F 18, G 18, D 18, E 18, D 19, E 19, D 16, F 19, B 19, A 18, B 18, A 17, D 14, C 18, B 17, C 19, B 16, or F 17, G 17, F 18, G 18, D 18, F 18, D 19, E 19, D 16, F 19, B 19, C 18, B 18.
19. Q 15, Q 14, R 15, S 15, T 16, S 14, Q 19, T 17, S 18, N 19, R 19.
20. T 3, S 6, T 5, S 3, R 3.
21. A 16, A 17, A 15, B 18, B 19, B 17, A 18, A 19, C 19.
22. C 3, B 3, B 2, B 1, A 2, A 3, B 6, B 5, A 5, A 1, D 4, B 4, B 8, E 1, B 9.

23. S 1, T 2, T 3, P 1, Q 1, Q 2, Q 3, R 1, R 2.
24. T 17, S 15, R 19.

II. KILLING GROUPS

1. Q 19, S 18, T 17, T 16, R 19, S 19, T 18, P 19, Q 19.
2. S 2, Q 4, O 5, R 3, R 1, S 1, T 1, S 3, T 4, T 3, S 4, or S 2, R 1, R 4, R 3, Q 4, S 4, S 3.
3. B 19, C 19, C 18, A 19, A 17.
4. A 1, D 1, B 1.
5. B 1, B 2, A 1, E 1, C 1.
6. C 14, E 18, C 18, E 17, B 17, C 16, A 17, A 16, B 19 or C 14, C 18, E 18, B 18, C 16, C 17, A 16, A 15, A 17, B 15, C 19, B 19, A 18 or C 14, C 18, E 18, C 16, B 19, C 19, B 18, B 15, A 15.
7. S 18, R 18, S 19, R 19, S 17, R 17, S 15.
8. T 5, T 4, R 4, S 4, S 2, S 3, T 2.
9. B 2, A 2, C 2, D 1, A 4, A 3, A 5, B 3, B 1, D 4, C 1 or B 2, B 3, C 2, D 1, A 2, B 1, A 4, A 3, D 4.
10. A 15, A 17, D 18, C 16, A 16, B 16, B 18 or A 15, B 16, D 18.
11. R 19, P 14, O 13, O 17, N 18, R 17, P 19.
12. T 2, T 5, T 3, Q 1, S 2, R 3, S 1, or T 2, T 5, T 3, S 2, Q 1, R 1, T 1.
13. F 1, D 1, A 3, A 2, B 1, C 1, G 1, B 2, D 2, C 2, E 1.
14. L 18, G 18, H 19, D 18, E 19 or L 18, D 18, F 18, G 18, F 17, E 18, H 18.
15. S 17, S 16, S 19, R 18, S 18, T 18, T 17, T 16, Q 19, R 19, P 19.
16. S 3, S 2, S 4, T 2, O 2, P 1, R 1, R 2, S 1.
17. B 19, B 18, E 19, C 18, B 15.
18. R 1, N 2, O 3, O 1, M 1, M 2, Q 1, L 2, N 1, L 1, N 1, M 1, T 3, T 2, T 4,
19. S 18, T 17, R 17, R 18, T 18, Q 17, T 16, R 17, P 18.

III. PLAYING FOR "KO"

1. S 18, T 16, T 17.
2. P 1, O 2, T 2, T 3, Q 2, Q 3, R 3, S 2, R 1, T 1, N 2 or P 1, Q 1, Q 3, Q 2, S 2, T 2, S 1, R 3, O 2 or P 1, S 2, O 2, Q 1, S 6, S 8, R 5, R 8, Q 3, Q 2, T 3, T 2, S 1.
3. A 18, C 19, B 19.
4. D 1, B 2, B 3, A 3, A 2, A 1, B 1.

5. A 2, B 2, A 3, E 1, B 1.

6. B 18, D 19, C 19.

7. T 18, S 18, P 19, T 19, Q 19.

8. S 2, T 4, T 3.

9. C 3, C 2, B 1, A 2, E 1, F 1, F 2, E 2, G 1, A 4, C 1, D 1.

10. A 18, A 17, B 19

11. P 19, T 17, T 18, S 19, R 19, R 18, Q 18 or P 19, R 19, S 19, S 18, T 19
    or P 19, S 18, T 18, R 18, Q 18, R 19, S 19.

12. R 1, S 3, T 1.

13. C 1, D 2, A 1.

14. B 14, B 13, B 18, A 14, A 17, C 18, A 15, B 15, B 16.

15. R 18, R 16, S 19, T 18, T 17, P 19, Q 19.

16. Q 3, P 2, S 5.

IV. Reciprocal Attacks ("Semeai")

1. S 19.

2. S 4, R 4, R 5, T 4, T 2, T 3; T 6.

3. B 18, D 19, B 19, C 19, F 19.

4. B 1.

5. B 1, A 2, F 1.

6. A 18.

7. T 18, R 19, R 16, S 16, S 15, S 14, P 17.

8. S 2, R 2, T 3.

9. B 2, A 2, B 1, C 1, C 3, A 1, B 2, B 1, B 5.

10. A 16, A 17, B 18.

11. S 2, S 3, R 2, T 2, S 1.

12. T 12, T 11, S 10.

V. Connecting Groups

1. O 15, N 16, M 15, O 14, O 17 or O 15, P 15, P 18, Q 18, P 16, O 17,
    O 18, Q 17, O 14.

2. T 5, T 6, S 6, T 4, Q 5, Q 6, P 7, O 7, O 5, Q 7, R 5, Q 4, R 5, Q 5,
    T 3.

3. E 15, E 16, B 17, B 16, D 16, C 15, A 16.

4. F 5, E 6, E 2, F 2, E 4, D 4, E 3, D 2, D 1.

5. F 4, E 4, F 3, E 3, F 2.

6. A 15, A 16, B 16, A 14, C 15.

7. Q 1, S 4, R 1, O 3, N 1, O 2, O 1.

8. S 15, T 15, S 14, R 16, Q 15, R 14, P 14.

9. J 2, H 2, H 1, J 3, K 3, H 4, G 1, F 2, F 1.

10. F 12, F 11, D 11, E 11, B 17, B 18, B 11, B 12, A 12, B 13, B 14, A 13, D 12.

11. L 16, M 15, M 18, L 18, M 17, L 17, L 19.

12. S 8, S 7, T 7, R 8, Q 7, S 9, R 9, R 6, T 8, Q 6, T 5 or S 8, S 7, T 7, R 8, Q 7, R 9, S 9, T 6, Q 6.

VI. " Oi otoshi "

1. T 18, T 19, R 19.

2. S 2, S 1, T 2, T 3, Q 1, T 1, S 2.

3. B 19, A 19, A 17, A 15, E 18.

4. A 2, A 1, A 4, A 5, D 1.

5. C 2, B 2, B 1, C 1, A 2.

6. B 19, C 19, C 17, A 19, B 18, B 19, A 17.

7. S 3, S 2, R 2, T 3, Q 2, S 3, T 5, Q 8, T 7, S 9, S 1, Q 7, T 2.

8. T 15, T 14, T 18, S 19, T 17, T 19, T 17, T 18, R 19, S 11, T 17, S 17.

9. H 1, G 7, E 1, F 1, D 1.

10. B 15, A 15, A 13, A 14, A 17.

11. M 17, L 17, N 19, M 19, L 18, K 18, K 19, L 19, J 19.

12. T 3, S 5, T 4.

VII. Cutting

1. G 16, F 16, G 14, F 14, F 15.

2. N 6, M 6, O 6, M 7, M 4.

3. G 16, F 16, G 14, H 15, F 15.

4. K 6, J 6, L 6, J 8, F 4.

GLOSSARY

Atari, a term used to warn an opponent when a player is about to surround completely a stone or a group of stones of his opponent. This is an old rule not always observed nowadays.

Daidaigeima (see also *Keima, Ogeima*), the placing of stones on the board in relation to each other like the Knight's move in Chess, but with the stones two spaces farther apart. See Plate 13, Diagram VII.

Dame, isolated "Me" on the frontier lines left on the board at the end of a game, which are of no importance to either player. See pp. 44–47.

Furin, the four-stone handicap which is given in addition to the ordinary nine-stone handicap. See Plate 12.

Go ban, the board on which the game of Go is played.

Go tsubo, the wooden jar that holds the Go stones, or "Ishi."

Ichi ban, winning a game by from one to ten "Me."

Ikken taka hiraki, an opening play or "Joseki" invented by Murase Shuho. See Plate 19 (C), Move 2.

Ikken taka kakari, an opening play or "Joseki" used in Examples XV (p. 134) and XIX (p. 138) in the chapter on "Joseki."

Ishi or *Go ishi,* the stones used in playing the game of Go.

Ji dori go, a contemptuous epithet meaning "ground taking Go," used in reference to the type of game in which the players concentrate on capturing space on the board without any regard to each other's plays.

Jo zu, the honorary title for players who have attained the rank of Seventh Degree Go player.

Joseki, the first stones placed on the board by a player. These opening moves are very important in determining the success of a player.

Kagome, the situation in which there appear to be, but actually are not, two disconnected "Me" in a player's group of stones which prevent the group from being taken. See pp. 33–34 and Plate 3, Diagram III.

Kakari (*Ikken kakari, Nikken kakari, Sangen kakari,* etc.), terms used to describe the placing of stones of opposite colors on the board in such a way that they are separated by one, two or three, etc., vacant spaces. See Plate 13, Diagram IV.

Kake tsugu, the placing of a stone in such a position that it effectively guards a point of connection between other stones, without actually connecting them as in the case of "Tsugu."

Kan shu, the honorary title for players who have attained the rank of Eighth Degree, the literal meaning of which is "the half-way step."

Keima (see also *Ogeima, Daidaigeima*), the placing of stones on the board in relation to each other similar to the Knight's move in Chess. Also called "Kogeima." See Plate 13, Diagram V.

Kiri kaeshi, one of the more common opening moves. See Plate 19 (B), Move 3.

Kiru, the playing of a stone in such a way that it prevents one's opponent from connecting up two or more of his own stones. See Plate 13, Diagram XIII.

Ko, the situation in which a player may not place a stone on a particular vacant intersection. For explanation See pp. 40–42.

Kogeima, see *Keima.*

Kogeima kakari, the placing of stones of different colors on the board in relation to each other like the Knight's move in Chess. This is the most usual move for attacking the corner. See Plate 19 (A), Move 1.

Komoku, the most usual and most conservative method of commencing the corner play at C 4 or D 3. See Plate 24 (A), Move 1.

Kosumu, the playing of a stone on the intersection diagonally adjacent to another stone.

Me, the points at which the lines of a Go board intersect and on which the stones are played. Also called "Moku." The literal meaning of the word is "eye." See pp. 31–32 for explanation of the principle of the two "Me."

Me wo tsukuru, an expression used to describe the processs whereby stones are finally arranged on the board to facilitate the counting.

Mei shu or *Meijin,* the honorary title for players who attain the rank of Ninth Degree, the literary meaning of which is "Celebrated man."

Moku, see *Me.*

Moku hadzushi, the least conservative of three usual openings, which is at E 3 or C 5. See Illustrative Game I, Move 1.

Naka oshi gatchi, a victory by a large margin in the early part of a game.

Naka yotsu, the four stone handicap which is given, usually only to the merest novice, in addition to the regular nine-stone handicap and the extra four-stone "Furin" handicap. See Plate 12.

Nikken take kakari, a form of opening or "Joseki" illustrated on Plate 20 (D), Move 3 and on Plate 21 (C), Move 1.

Nobiru, extending a line of stones by placing another in the adjacent vacant "Me" and not skipping a space as in the case of "Ikken tobi." See Plate 13, Diagram XIV.

Nozoku, the playing of a stone in such a way that it prevents an opponent from completely surrounding a "Me." See Plate 13, Diagram VIII. The term is also applied to the playing of a stone as a preliminary move in cutting the connection between two of the adversary's stones or groups of stones. See pp. 62–63.

Ogeima, the placing of stones on the board in relation to each other like the Knight's move in Chess, but with the stones one space farther apart. See Plate 13, Diagram VI.

Ogeima kakari, a form of opening play or "Joseki" in which a player does not attack a corner directly but gets a better chance on the sides or center. See Plate 20 (C), Move 1.

Ogeima shimari, a form of opening play or "Joseki" that is supposed to be a strong formation protecting a corner. See Example XXIV (p. 142) in the chapter on "Joseki."

Oi otoshi, a sudden and unexpected attack by a player who is protecting an area, carried out by forcing the adversary to take certain stones and in doing so to be obliged to abandon part of his surrounding chain in order not to sustain greater losses.

Osaeru, the playing of a stone in such a way that it prevents one's adversary from continuing a line of stones. See Plate 13, Diagram XV.

Ozaru, the relationship of two stones near the edge of the board which gains about eight spaces. See Example XVII (p. 136) in the chapter on "Joseki."

Seimoku, the nine intersections on a Go board on which handicap stones are placed. They are marked with black dots.

Seki, the situation in which a vacant space is surrounded partly by white and partly by black stones in such a way that, if either player places a stone therein, his adversary can thereupon capture the entire group. See Plate 6, Diagram VI.

Semeai, an encounter between one who is attacking an area and a defender attempting to capture the stones which are being used by his adversary in the attack.

Sente, the situation in which a player is taking the lead in a certain part of the board, compelling his adversary to answer his moves or else sustain greater damage. See p. 62.

Shicho, the situation in which two players carry on a running attack, forming a zigzag pattern across the board. See Plate 13, Diagram IX.

Shiki ishi, additional handicap stones.

Shogi, the Japanese form of chess, which is slightly different from the game as played in other countries.

Sute ishi, stones which are sacrificed in order to kill a larger group. The literal meaning is "thrown away stones."

Takamoku, an opening play at E 4 or D 5, which is the most aggressive of the three usual methods of opening. See Plate 22 (D), Move 1.

Takamoku kakari, a form of opening or "Joseki" that is one of the two most often used general methods of replying to "Moku hadzushi."

Te okure, an unnecessary or wasted move or one that is not the best possible. See pp. 65–66.

Ten gen, the central spot on the board on which the fifth handicap stone is placed.

Tenuki, shifting from one area of combat to another in a different part of the board.

Tobi (Ikken tobi, Nikken tobi, Sangen tobi, etc.), terms used to describe the placing of one's stones in such a way that they are separated by one, two, three, etc., vacant spaces. See Plate 13, Diagrams I–III.

Tsugu, a move made to connect two or more stones previously played. See Plate 13, Diagram XII.

Tsuke te, an opening move shown in Plate 19 (D), Move 2.

Ute kaeshi, a sitsuation that resembles "Ko," but actually is not one in which the rule of "Ko" is applied. The literal meaning is "returning a blow." For explanation, see p. 42 and Plate 6, Diagrams III–V.

Watari, the making of a connection between two groups of stones, usually near the edge of the board. See Plate 13, Diagram X.